Affirmations of a Dissenter

C. Joseph Sprague

ABINGDON PRESS
Nashville ·

AFFIRMATIONS OF A DISSENTER

Copyright © 2002 by Abingdon Press

Library of Congress Cataloging-in-Publication Data

Sprague, C. Joseph, 1939–
    Affirmations of a dissenter / [C. Joseph Sprague].
        p.   cm.
    ISBN 0-687-72825-8 (pbk. : alk. paper)
    1. United Methodist Church (U.S.)—Doctrines.   2. Methodist
Church—Doctrines.   I. Title.
    BX8331.3 .S67   2002
    287'.6—dc21

2002011313

03 04 05 06 07 08 09 10 11 — 10 9 8 7 6 5 4

MANUFACTURED IN THE UNITED STATES OF AMERICA

Acknowledgments

✝ ✝ ✝

Innumerable colleagues have given time, energy, and critical guidance to make this book possible. Having written countless sermons aimed at the ear, readers like Pamela Couture, Ronald G. Payne, Martha Scott, Linda and Wayne Rhodes, and, most particularly, the indefatigable Thomas Sagendorf, goaded me to write this offering, to the degree an old dog can learn new tricks, for the eye. I acknowledge their critical insights, which are gifts of our abiding friendship and shared journeys. While I take full responsibility for the content of the following pages, this project would not have come to fruition without these trusted advisors.

The completion of most writing projects is made possible by unseen and unsung persons who give unstintingly of themselves on behalf of the author's efforts. This book is no exception. My cherished friend, Jan Lichtenwalter, journalist, poet, and lay theologian, provided adroit insights and corrective editing. Phyllis Griffin, my indomitable administrative assistant, transcribed more scribbled pages and subsequent corrections than anyone should be asked to decipher. She did so willingly, ably, and with her usual winsome spirit. To these two I remain profoundly grateful—even when they team up to make fun of my terrible penmanship and wordy proclivities.

Contents

✝   ✝   ✝

Introduction

✝ ✝ ✝

The title of this book emerged from within me during the 1990s. If I were to write a piece longer and more comprehensive than Sunday sermons and weekly columns for parish or conference newspapers, it would reflect the dialectic between faith affirmation and institutional dissent.

The longer I live—and I am now Social Security eligible—the stronger grows my trust in and commitment to God's hospitable and unconditional love. But paradoxically, the deeper this faith becomes, the more uncomfortable I am with some of the trends found in religious institutions, particularly in the denomination I know best.

Thus, what follows is a composite of affirmation and dissent, of faith and protest, of that which I joyfully affirm and that against which I must protest. This paradoxical piece flows from the heart and mind of a bishop who affirms the church's calling but finds some of its present tendencies to be out of step with the teachings of Jesus and the witness of the Risen Christ whose presence calls us to discipleship.

I do not write to answer my critics; I suspect that this work will only increase the fury of some. Rather, I write especially for those on the way who need kindred voices, honest minds, welcoming hearts, and the gift of candor to "keep on keeping on" in a church that often talks about Jesus, but fails to be the institutional expression of that One whose hospitality was inclusive and universal.

This book is dedicated to my spouse of forty-three years, Diane, who has shared most of my affirmations and faced courageously and unstintingly the consequences of all my dissents, and to the memory of the late Van Bogard Dunn, who pointed me on the way with intellectual vigor, consummate courage, and unquenchable faith. Additionally, this offering is for all who affirm Jesus as Liberator and Savior, but who are vexed in the deepest recesses of their souls with the attempted takeover of the church by closed minds and fearful hearts, which seek security in rigid literalism, narrow parochialism, and hurtful exclusivism.

I affirm Jesus as Savior and Liberator, but I dissent from much that is said, done, and not done in his name in today's church.

Chapter One

A Tough Mind and a Tender Heart

Martin Luther King, Jr.'s insightful sermon based on Jesus' instruction to the Twelve in Matthew 10:16—"See, I am sending you out like sheep into the midst of wolves; so be wise as serpents [tough-minded] and innocent as doves [tender-hearted]"—put my faith journey and vocational calling into perspective when I first read it in King's book *Strength to Love* while a seminarian in the early 1960s.

Raised a Quaker in a theologically conservative congregation and yearly meeting, I benefited from the caring nurture of those affirming Friends, and a wonderfully loving home of origin, that marked me early as one who knew from experience the reality of God's unconditional love. My parents, extended family, and the pastor of that Dayton Friends Meeting, Billy Lewis, his spouse, Marie, and the embracing people of that tiny congregation were conduits for grace upon grace for an inner-city youngster from a rural migrant family. I honor the gifts they bestowed upon me. I shudder to imagine what I would have become without them.

Yet, as adolescence dawned, I began to question the literal approach to scripture. Additionally, my soul was restless with the disconnection I sensed, but could not yet describe, between the welcoming, hospitable creed of Jesus' words and the inactions and hurtful daily deeds that were readily apparent all around me. People I loved labeled, categorized, and excluded immigrant children whose parents talked differently, southerners who went "down home" each weekend and, most of all, black people, like my teammates on our superb seventh-grade basketball team at Roosevelt Junior and Senior High School on Dayton, Ohio's near west side.

We were the Roosevelt Teddy Bears, the mighty Teddies. There was a popular hangout near the school that served memorable hamburgers, spicy barbecue, soggy french fries with thick gravy, ice cold Pepsi Cola, and incomparable potato chips. It was there that God initially called me to ordained ministry, and it was there that my young and tender heart began to long for a much needed tough mind. It happened like this.

Following a basketball game in late December 1951, a teammate and I went for a snack. I ordered a Pepsi and a bag of chips. Sanford Davis, my companion, asked for the same. The man rang up a ten-cent sale for me and grabbed my dime with an unaccustomed scowl. Sanford gave this man, who I had experienced as friendly to youngsters, a half dollar. The man pounded the keys of his cash register and the announcement of a fifty cent sale popped before our eyes. I was astounded. Ten cents for me, but fifty cents for Sanford. And for the same two items! I started to protest, my innocence rapidly vanishing. But Sanford intervened. It was 1951, and he knew the score. "It's okay, Joe. This happens to us all the time."

It was then that I heard God say in my heart of hearts: *Joe, I want you to spend your life seeing that people who look like Sanford (who was African American) are not treated as Sanford just was and that people who look like you and the man behind the counter don't treat others as your friend and teammate was just treated.*

My tender heart was broken, and a mind not yet tough began to churn. The churning has not ceased. How can there be in Christian America, as we were taught our nation was, such a disparity between creed and deed, words of love and actions of bigotry? And where was the church, as countless Sanfords and Samanthas were treated so cruelly? If the words and stories of Jesus were true, why were believers, who testified and prayed twice on Sunday and regularly at Wednesday night prayer meetings, not saying and doing what Jesus clearly practiced and expected of his followers? Increasingly, I became dismayed and confused.

If this were not enough for an adolescent to digest, my plate of intellectual questioning began to fill as I sought to make sense of familiar stories from the Bible in the midst of challenging lessons gleaned at school and hard realities absorbed from the streets.

Predictably, I started a free fall away from both the church I loved and from the Bible whose stories had played a crucial role in my moral and spiritual development. If personal testimonies were not lived out in daily life, what power did they hold? If creation did not really happen in six days, if Jonah could not live in the belly of a big fish or get there without being chewed up, or if dead bodies did not come back to life, despite the prayers of the faithful, how could the Bible be true?

God had called me to ordained ministry. I sensed this. But how could I say "Yes" when I did not see Jesus being followed or his teachings enacted? Jesus was affirmed in the church, yes. Followed daily, no. Besides this, treasured biblical stories made less and less sense to an inquisitive, yet deeply pietistic and rigidly moralistic, adolescent. My heart had been warmed by God in countless Quaker Meetings, summer camps, and at the altar rail of a revival meeting, but my mind was cold—except for questions too hot to ask in the 1950s church.

I did not know it then, but I would learn later that out of this existential crisis would emerge the paradox that would shape my ministry and the credo that would guide my life. King's sermon named it well: "A Tough Mind and a Tender Heart."

It is this paradoxical tension, with which I have lived for fifty years, that both drives the affirmations and fuels the dissents that follow.

Conclusion

The tough mind and tender heart combine the essentials of personal piety and the prophetic tradition. These elements are at the heart of United Methodism's historic commitments to internal nurture of the individual and external involvement in informed missional and social justice ministries.

I affirm that the mature Christian and a vital church must exemplify the confluence of these two historic, even paradoxical, components of faithful discipleship.

Chapter Two

Bible Stories We Had Not Heard

My parents had moved our family from the inner-city neighborhood, near Roosevelt Junior and Senior High School, to a nearby suburb when I entered eighth grade. And while I met Diane there (my beloved friend, treasured life partner of forty-three years, and the mother of our five children) and while several remarkable enduring friendships developed in that suburban setting, I was quietly enraged that my parents would dare to move me from the neighborhood I knew so well and the Teddy Bear identity I cherished.

In retrospect, I came to see that, because my report cards through grade seven were a source of family pride, in typical passive-aggressive fashion I silently ceased being an exceptional student after we moved. I had decided to show them. In fact I cannot recall taking home one book during my final five years of public school. Instead I filled my time with athletics, girls, automobiles, and odd jobs.

Despite the expectation that I would be the first in the extended family to go to college, I nearly flunked out of college the first semester. I was unprepared academically and emotionally for this life transition. And my first semester grades proved it. Fortunately, as luck would have it, a supposed mishap of scheduling placed me in advanced English composition as the second semester opened. In that setting, ill-prepared and painfully aware of it, I encountered Richard Snyder, a demanding teacher, who, having just completed a doctoral dissertation on James Joyce, did not suffer fools gladly. And I was just such a fool. He knew it and so did I. But "The Duke," as we called him, rekindled my fire for learning. He demanded that I think, read, and write. Given the chord he struck within me, I took every elective he offered during my final three years of college. This was a time of accelerated growth, intellectual excitement, and modest achievement—so much so that either law or graduate school was in the offing as college graduation loomed.

Despite the excitement of it all, I felt little enthusiasm for either the practice of law or the pursuit of an academic degree. Something else, some unspoken passion had claimed me. This imponderable, along with the tangible reality of a growing family, preempted immediate formal study following college graduation. Instead, I worked full time at the sales and sales management job I had held as a college junior and senior. Selling cutlery was a satisfactory means to the end of paying college expenses while supporting our family, but for me it was a miserable end in and of itself. I felt a bit like Willy Loman at the tender age of twenty-two.

There, in the awful loneliness of feeling trapped by circumstance, reeling a bit out of customary control, far from God (or so I assumed) and the church I silently had repudiated in successive waves of agnosticism, atheism, and glib dismissal of institutional irrelevance, I began to sense anew the tenacious mystique of God's call that had claimed me years before in the Teddy Bear Restaurant. "Over here, over here. I want you over here," the inaudible but relentless voice intoned. Diane also was at loose ends. With her typical support anchored in intuitive insight regarding the state of my troubled soul and our weakening relationship, she suggested a return to the church. Perhaps what was missing within and between us was a renewed relationship with God (whatever this meant). Maybe the emptiness would be filled if we returned to the church. After all, it had been formative for both of us in our earlier years.

Again, as luck would have it (the recurrent pun in the book of Ruth where not luck but God's Providence is operative), while I was scanning the yellow pages late one Saturday night in order to locate a church near our apartment—bingo!—there it was, a Methodist church only a few blocks away. Off to church we went the next morning. I do not pretend to remember what Paul Acker said that day, but his sermon and demeanor struck a resonant chord.

The following Sunday, when he made a request for a volunteer to teach a junior high Sunday school class, Diane nudged me, saying, "You can do that." I did. Within six weeks the call to ordained ministry was answered, and we became Methodists. Almost immediately, the search for a seminary began. Again, dear Ruth, as luck would have it, that Methodist congregation had a student pastor on staff. Walter Hayes was a member of the first class of students at the brand new Methodist Theological School in Ohio (MTSO). Walt would not take no for an answer. I was going to visit MTSO with him, no matter what. "Forget those East Coast schools," he said. "Believe me, this is the place for you."

It was! One of those life-defining moments occurred when Walt ushered me into the dean's office and introduced me to Van Bogard Dunn. I did not know it then, but over the ensuing years Bogie would become my teacher, role model, elder brother, coconspirator, colleague, and treasured friend. At that moment I did know that I was home at last, and that God had brought me to a place where there was at least one person who embodied the nascent hopes and dreams that were bottled within me. Bogie epitomized keen intellect, quick wit, raw courage, indefatigable energy, no-nonsense piety, and electrifying charisma, all packaged in a vital human being of accessible faith ready to be experienced. I wanted at least a piece of what Bogie represented.

Therefore, in the fall of 1962, having been a Methodist for only five months and a student pastor for three, I became a seminarian at MTSO, class of 1965. Again, Providence shined. The class of 1965 was populated with kindred spirits, young men who were pietistic, intellectually hungry, socially and politically awakening, and irreverent. Yet, like me, they were deeply hopeful for the emergence of a Church that would be a bold expression of faithfulness and radical commitment.

The faculty of the new seminary was a wild and wonderful amalgam of veterans who had come out of retirement to anchor the school and raw rookies who were eager to sail against every ill wind. They were serene and brash, arrogant and patient, mature and naive, not unlike many of their students. There was no theological party line at MTSO in 1962. But neither was the school a hiding place for biblical literalists nor closet fundamentalists. The rigor of academic life, incarnational realities of student parishes, and the societal conflicts of the early 1960s, precluded any soft-headedness or hard-heartedness.

Fred D. Gealy, a wizened giant among the faculty, former missionary, linguist, musician, theologian, and New Testament scholar of world renown, who was steeped in the demythologizing methodology of Rudolf Bultmann, put it all into perspective when he opened his New Testament class session with these words, "Come boys [unfortunately, seminary students were all males in those years], and I'll teach you Bible stories you have never heard."

And he and his colleagues did just that. I had utterly rejected the biblical literalism of my childhood and was unable to embrace the god of classical theism I had abandoned as an adolescent because I could not correlate unfair suffering, particularly the deaths of children, with a Big Daddy up there somewhere controlling it all. I went to seminary as a blank theological slate, eager to have written on my being insights and methodologies that would give expression to my growing spirituality and speak truth to a church badly in need of relevance, if the world were to be served for Jesus' sake.

I was not disappointed. Seminary was a joy ride. I studied and integrated the learnings eagerly. The work of the twentieth century giants in theology, biblical studies, social ethics, and the practical disciplines fed my soul. And for most of us in the class of 1965, our classroom learnings were tested, tempered, and integrated through the civil rights and anti-war movements of that turbulent era. A treasured gift of the seminary years was the recovery of the Bible I had discovered as a child in Quaker Meeting. Through the various schools of biblical criticism, the Bible came alive again. I learned to read it expectantly, metaphorically, contextually and, in part, poetically without falling victim to the idolatry of biblical literalism. The discovery of the Word beyond the human but inspired words of Holy Scripture was a rare epiphany. And, I came to understand and affirm the Bible as the primary source of revelation and authority for both the church and my life and ministry. Ed Meyer taught us that there is no preaching other than biblical preaching, in which text and context meet in the vulnerability, candor, and prayerful hard work of the preacher who dares to speak saying, "Thus says the Lord. . . ." Because of Ed, biblical theology and expository preaching became the hallmarks of my vocational journey and remain a driving passion to this day.

While God was never declared dead at MTSO or from any pulpit behind which I stood, surely the god of classical theism—an essentially male, impregnating Being out there somewhere, who either started it all and backed off or who controls it by indistinguishable behavior altered occasionally, even miraculously, by certain prayers and supernatural interventions—was dead because that god never really existed except in the minds of the fanciful or superstitious. Thankfully, my seminary years provided an awareness of other powerful and inviting images of God that were emerging; that time also introduced me to theological thinking that not only makes sense, but also correlates life and faith for real people in a real and broken but hopeful world.

Seminary, with its traditional curriculum of Bible, theology, church history, and the practical disciplines of preaching, Christian education, pastoral care, and church administration, along with its communal life based on a collective commitment to the motto of MTSO, "To Preach the Word," and its unswerving involvement in civil rights, the anti-war movement, and an intentional effort to renew the institutional church at every level, was for me a seminal period. I affirm quality, relevant theological education as a gift of God for the people of God. It was for me.

There in seminary in the 1960s, during that wonderfully chaotic, if traumatic time, while sitting at the feet of great teachers, I was radicalized, taken to the root of my being where God in Christ already had called me by name. MTSO equipped me to answer that call by providing adaptable tools that have been employed for forty years in the practice of ministry in various settings.

My seminary education helped immeasurably to renew my relationship with Christ, to reaffirm the fundamentals of the Christian movement, and to make sense of the rich tradition that undergirds the church in all of its frailty and dysfunctionality. Those formative years gave the Bible back to me as its stories and wondrous affirmations of God's unconditional love became conduits for what the Spirit sought to do with me and to say to the church in our time.

Because I heard and believed biblical and other faith stories I had not heard previously, seminary made possible a lifelong affirmation of God in Christ and made necessary institutional and societal dissent.

Conclusion

I believe that the providence of God is operative in mysterious ways, creating opportunities for each of us. Much is given as possibility. Each of us has the human capacity through faithful response to link our destinies with what God has provided. The confluence of such grace and faith provides the possibility for the unexpected to occur.

I affirm that my experience at MTSO, particularly the re-entry into the power of the biblical witness, was the result of the confluence of Providence and the faithful response of many people. As luck would have it, that confluence made a renewed affirmation of God in Christ possible while demanding that I dissent from all that is less than what God desires for the whole created order.

It is to such affirmative dissent that I now turn.

Chapter Three

The Issue Is Biblical Authority

Talk for any length of time with Christians who represent polar opposite positions on the homosexual controversy that divides the Christian community, regardless of denomination, and you will discover that both sides agree on one thing: the real issue is biblical authority.

The more conservative proponents of the present positions within United Methodism regarding gay and lesbian Christians adamantly assert that their stance is biblically based and that any liberalizing of the Church's policies on ordination, union services, or the "practice" of homosexuality would strike at the root of biblical teaching. To buttress this position, proponents in this camp point to seven passages of scripture where they believe homosexuality is condemned.

Progressives, on the other hand, suggest that Jesus is not recorded as having spoken on this subject. They are quick to ask others to examine closely the biblical passages in question in their actual contextual settings. The Genesis story about Sodom (from which comes *sodomy*) is interpreted to be understood more accurately as an example of gross inhospitality rather than a condemnation of same-sex orientation or behavior. Most progressives dismiss the codes in Leviticus as time-bound laws for a certain era. The words of Paul in 1 Corinthians 6 and Romans 1 are interpreted as protests against sexual immorality in all forms, opposition to the gross manipulation of others, especially children; disavowal of the misuse of power; and the unnatural acts of heterosexuals behaving as if they were homosexuals. Progressives say that the Bible knows nothing of inherent sexual orientation, only deviant behavior. They believe that from Genesis to Revelation the trajectory of the biblical witness is God's inclusive love that calls all of humankind into covenant with the Holy One through the hospitable and God-manifesting witness and life of the people of the Covenant, namely, Israel and the church.

I shall address the homosexual issue more specifically in a subsequent chapter, but for now my reference to this issue puts before us, in graphic contrast, one of the two fundamental and highly divisive issues in the church today, namely, the nature of biblical authority. The second highly divisive issue is Christology, and that, too, shall be discussed later.

Sitting on the progressive side of the biblical and theological divide, I have been both angered and saddened that biblical conservatives, whom I am calling neoliteralists given their inconsistent literal reading of scripture, and their caucus groups[1] have assumed that they are the only Christians who are faithful to biblical authority. Their message is that they represent scriptural Christianity and the rest of us do not.

Thus, in part angry at past nearly slanderous allegations made against me by some neoliteralists regarding my approach to the Bible, deeply saddened by the way the Bible is being treated by neoliteralism (as if more than a century of biblical scholarship is for naught), and troubled profoundly that neoliteralism is assumed widely in church and culture to be the rightful methodology for interpreting scripture, I intend in this chapter to dissent unapologetically from this nearly unchallenged takeover

---

1. As I write, these groups are Good News, the Confessing Movement, and the Institute for Religion and Democracy (IRD).

of the biblical high ground. I do strongly affirm that the Bible is and ever shall be the primary source of authority for all Christians and that biblical authority must not be viewed as static truth that falls off the pages of the Bible. Instead, it is a dynamic process that is empowered by the work of the Holy Spirit in the midst of the faith community's discernment processes through prayer, dialogue, informed scholarship, and application to the issues of today.

My dissent as a United Methodist includes incredulity that neoliteralism has been permitted, with little sustained challenge to the contrary from many who know better, to take passages out of context and read a particular theology into them. To the detriment of the whole church, in failing to foster informed debate on biblical authority, progressives have been lax in calling neoliteralists to task. Neoliteralists have been allowed to pick and choose certain texts to buttress their own predisposed positions in the name of scriptural Christianity.

I do hereby dissent from the arrogance of neoliteralism and the cowardly silence of progressives. In dissenting, I ask these questions of the neoliteralists. Given your stance on homosexuality, how do you read the words of Jesus on matters related to divorce and remarriage? The taking of human life whether in war or by capital punishment? The gradual, but apparent acceptance of women as leaders in the church? By posing these questions I presuppose that the neoliteralistic methodology demands consistency in biblical interpretation and that the neoliteralists are far from consistent in their interpretation, application, and use of Holy Scripture. Let me be specific.

I do not recall an orchestrated effort from the many neoliteralists at the 2000 General Conference when United Methodism affirmed almost unanimously in the Social Principles, "When a married couple is estranged beyond reconciliation, even after thoughtful consideration and counsel, divorce is a regrettable alternative in the midst of brokenness. . . . Divorce does not preclude a new marriage" (Paragraph 161.D).

My point is not that I disagree with our Church on divorce and remarriage or that our position is not justifiable biblically. Rather, my question is how can the neoliteralists mount the campaign they have with regard to the supposed biblical mandate regarding homosexuality (when the Bible's position is murky at best on this subject) and overlook the words of Jesus regarding divorce and remarriage? The oldest of the Gospel accounts, Mark, records Jesus as saying, "Whoever divorces his wife and marries another commits adultery against her; and if she divorces her husband and marries another she commits adultery" (Mark 10:10-12). At least Roman Catholicism and some of the unequivocally fundamental Protestant denominations are consistent. What is the biblical hermeneutic at work that allows articulate leaders of neoliteralism to turn their collective back on their own approach to scripture in one instance while attacking gay and lesbian persons in the other?

The same question holds true regarding the taking of human life. Jesus is clear in the Sermon on the Mount, as Matthew (5:38-44) records it, regarding the sacredness of human life. Matthew has Jesus say:

> "You have heard that it was said, 'An eye for an eye and a tooth for a tooth.' But I say to you, Do not resist an evildoer. But if anyone strikes you on the right cheek, turn the other also. . . . You have heard that it was said, 'You shall love your neighbor and hate your enemy.' But I say to you, Love your enemies and pray for those who persecute you."

How can neoliteralism be supportive of the present war? How can it write off the pursuit of nonviolent alternatives, given the words of Jesus? And, how can neoliteralists not advocate for the abolition of capital punishment, the curtailment of National Rifle Association–influenced gun availability, and a rethinking of this nation's reliance on military might if the words of Jesus in the Bible are to be taken at face value as neoliteralism demands? How can neoliteralism be pro-war and anti-homosexual, or anti-abortion and pro–capital punishment? Where is the consistency? What is the hermeneutical principle at work? And where is either the logic or the pastoral heart in this pick-and-choose approach to biblical authority? I dissent from what I believe is self-serving eisegesis.[2]

The same questions apply when we examine the role of women in leadership in the Church. To my delight, many women are in key positions of leadership in United Methodism. I rejoice that our North Central Jurisdiction College of Bishops includes four female bishops, who are among the intellectual and spiritual leaders of the Council of Bishops (COB). I view several of my female colleagues in the COB as among our denomination's finest episcopal leaders.

However, I can well remember, not only in the episcopal office but in matters of lay elections, ordination, and clergy promotions, when the voices of opposition toward women from the neoliteralists were boisterous, even strident. Now they would not be so bold. Is this because the words of the Bible have changed? Hardly. First Timothy still says unequivocally:

> Women should dress themselves modestly and decently in suitable clothing, not with their hair braided, or with gold, pearls, or expensive clothes, but with good works, as is proper for women who profess reverence for God. Let a

2. Eisegesis reads into the text what the readers want to hear instead of seeking to hear what the text actually meant in historic context.

woman learn in silence with full submission. *I permit no woman to teach or to have authority over a man; she is to keep silent.* For Adam was formed first, then Eve; and Adam was not deceived, but the woman was deceived and became a transgressor. Yet she will be saved through childbearing, provided they continue in faith and love and holiness, with modesty. (1 Timothy 2:9-15, italics added)

This passage presents a dramatic dilemma for neoliteralists as they now point proudly to women leaders in their midst.[3] That is, at face value, the 1 Timothy text about the place of women in leadership in the church (namely, nowhere) is clearly not being followed in their daily practices. What is the biblical hermeneutic at work that makes rather obscure biblical texts definitive and exclusive regarding homosexuality, while the unambiguous statement in 1 Timothy is either ignored or defied?

I question and dissent from the neoliteralists' inconsistent approach to the Bible that makes of scripture a theological and political cafeteria line that suits the political appetite of neoliteralists instead of inviting all of us to feast and be nurtured by the whole biblical offering.

To distance myself from the hermeneutical methodology of neoliteralism and to raise my voice of dissent regarding this shortsighted methodology and self-serving conclusions, it is incumbent upon me to make my affirmation of the biblical witness. I need to demonstrate how the Bible, complete with its inherent inconsistencies and time-bound understandings, truths and falsehoods, myths and poetry, prose and theological evolution, is the composite of Holy Spirit-inspired human words that point to the divine Word. That is, the Bible is the yeasty dough of human hands, raised by the work of the Holy Spirit in the church to be the

---

3. As I write, both the Confessing Movement and IRD have women in their top positions of executive leadership.

primary witness to the Bread of Life who is Jesus the Risen Christ, the Word become flesh.

To begin to do this, I invite you to consider the following illustration gleaned from the teaching of Fred D. Gealy, who forty years ago taught his students, "Bible stories we had hever heard."

Jesus is shown walking on the sea in Matthew 14 and Mark 6. How could this be? My understanding, and that of many others, of a fully human Jesus does not square with the supernatural power to cavort across a sea, especially during a turbulent storm. Something else, something deeper and more profound, is at work in these texts. Gealy opened wide the window of understanding on this story and helped me to begin to see deeper truth about Jesus and to better understand biblical revelation in all of its complex power.

He described in intricate detail the cosmology of the three-story universe taken for granted when Mark and Matthew wrote: (1) Above were the starry heavens—the abode of God; (2) Down below was Sheol—the place of utter darkness; and, (3) Betwixt and between was Earth where powers from Above and Below did battle for the kingdoms of this world and the souls of human beings. Between Sheol and Earth was stretched the Sea, not merely a body of water but the mythological abode of chaos where the great demons Leviathan and Behemoth, and even death itself, loomed. Thus, Jesus the Son came from Above (the Virgin Birth myth) to Earth to do cosmic battle with the powers and principalities of the underworld for the souls of humans and the sovereignty of the universe. Therefore, where else could God's preeminent representative walk but on the Sea where the enemy seemingly was in control? Jesus walked on chaos and death and defeated both along with all the powers and principalities. Is this not why Jesus drove the demon-filled swine back into the sea in Mark

5:13? Jesus is Savior and Sovereign. Death in any form is not the victor; but rather, the Victim is Victor!

I could say more. But in 1962 the biblical and theological insight and hermeneutical approach this example illustrates began to unlock the mystery of the Bible for me. I grew to realize that biblical authority is not found in selective proof-texting that announces, "The Bible says . . ." Rather, I learned that biblical authority has to do with the dynamic power of the Holy Spirit working through aged, time-bound human, but sacred writings, so that the words of the Bible become for the faith community, the primary microscope for seeing God's nearness and intimacy and the focused telescope for glimpsing God's otherness and grandeur. To see God's immanence and transcendence requires more than a surface reading of ancient words; much more is required.

Like so many (too many of whom have become strangely quiet as the neoliteralists have made the Bible their chastening rod), I learned and continue to practice the reading of the Bible through an exegetical methodology that always takes the context and placement of a particular text very seriously. When was this text written? To whom? Why? What is its literary form? What is its relationship to the larger body of material in which it is set? These are elementary questions to be asked as a particular biblical passage is approached. Progressive readers seek to understand the text in its ancient context and then attempt to interpret, translate, and correlate it with our present life situations. Such a methodology, best done in small groups, particularly in congregational study settings, is essential if the Bible is to be God's vehicle for the eternal Word to emerge beyond our finite words. Given such an understanding of biblical truth and the disciplined work of exegesis, the texts earlier cited in this chapter are heard and appropriated far differently by progressives than by neoliteralists.

It is to the task of progressive interpretation, of employing an informed and consistent hermeneutic, that I now turn.

Divorce

Let's begin by considering Mark's account of Jesus' hard saying about divorce and remarriage in Mark 10. Note that this text does not emerge from a vacuum. Contextually, we learn that once again the Pharisees are trying to entrap Jesus. Legalistic religion (controlled by privileged males who could do just about whatever they wanted with their wives, their female property, in the male-dominated paternalistic world of the Bible) was being employed to back Jesus into a corner. But Jesus would have none of the Pharisees' legalistic maneuvering. He confronted the powers and principalities hiding in hard-nosed religious rigidity, as they lurked surreptitiously posing as ethical faith.

"You think you are ethical, boys?" Jesus seemed to say, "Let me show you genuine marital ethics." Instead of privileged men being able to dismiss women as property at a whim or to have sexual intercourse with whomever they chose, so long as she was not the property of another male, Jesus set the record straight on marriage by taking his adversaries back to a portion of the creation stories found in Genesis 2:23-24. He pointed to God's intention for all married couples by revisiting this formative text about God's intended purposes for marriage in creation and by confronting the self-righteousness of the religious leaders. In so doing, quite radically, Jesus put women on par with the controlling males. He upset the patriarchal world of religious rigidity that manipulated and discarded women.

It is clear, Jesus affirmed, that God's intent, God's dream for humankind is that marriage be held sacrosanct. The two are one. The real issue in Mark's text, however, is not whether divorce is ever justifiable, but how the Pharisees were self-righteously admonishing others to do one thing while doing for themselves whatever served their own self-interest. In the story, Jesus saw through their ruse and confronted their hypocrisy. It becomes apparent that we do not have in Mark a new legalism about marriage and divorce but a refutation of rigid holier-than-thou self-righteousness.

Therefore, while divorce is always hurtful and wounds not only all parties involved, but also the very heart of God, reason and experience teach us that there are some situations where divorce clearly is the most loving and just option. In such cases the biblical God who does make all things new sanctions divorce and is involved as a nurturing and healing presence when a new marriage is begun.

I affirm the United Methodist position on marriage, divorce, and remarriage. It reflects the spirit and inherent truth of the biblical witness. I believe it conveys the heart and spirit of Jesus' teachings.

War and Violence

The words of Jesus, as recorded in the Gospels, are unequivocal. Over and over again, our Lord spoke against violence, for forgiveness, and on behalf of love. We may suggest he was naive or that he and the early church were advocating an interim-ethic, a radical short-lived lifestyle to be in vogue until Jesus returned, or that he was addressing interpersonal and not international matters. But no one can deny that Jesus was a pacifist in words, deeds, and lifestyle. What have neoliteralists done, and what can they do, with Jesus' example? Pretend it does not exist? Ignore it? Explain it away? If so, on this thorny issue about which Jesus spoke so often, how can neoliteralists pretend "scriptural Christianity" regarding their opposition to gay and lesbian Christians, when Jesus is not recorded as having spoken on the subject? I dissent from their self-serving inconsistency and affirm that whether we like it or not, Jesus taught and lived nonviolence and expected the same of his followers. The early church did so believe, considering that nearly four hundred years of pacifism followed the church's birth. I suspect that neoliteralists find clever ways to explain away the obvious they do not like, while straining considerably to make plain that which is nonexistent, which they do like.

Neoliteralists aside, as regards war and violence, I affirm that now is the time for us to recommit ourselves to follow Jesus. Our mission is to walk his talk as we hear Jesus say to us, "Blessed are the merciful, for they will receive mercy. Blessed are the pure in heart, for they will see God. Blessed are the peacemakers, for they will be called children of God" (Matthew 5:7-9).

Given Jesus' teachings about nonviolence across the pages of the Synoptics, I confess that I cannot understand how neoliteralists can be unequivocal supporters of the war in Afghanistan, pro–NRA, pro–capital punishment, and seemingly eager to treat United States military might as a modern god. Apparently neoliteralists feel comfortable with such an inconsistent, nonbiblical position, but I must raise my voice of dissent. Clearly, such a stance does not find credence in the life of the early church, the ministry of Jesus, or the witness of the Gospels. I say this partly because of the pacifism of the early church and primarily because of the witness of the New Testament, especially the recorded words of Jesus regarding the use of force. The unmistakable bias of these sources is pro-life and against any form of violence that threatens, let alone takes human life.

Yet, I know that I run the danger of embracing the very methodology from which I dissent if I only quote Jesus and refer to church history and assume that such assertions make my point. Therefore, I offer the following:

Where I live and work daily in the Chicago Area, the

effects of violence on the young (perpetuated at least in part by the availability of weapons of violence) cry out for redress. Needed are systemic solutions that would expose and erase the root causes of violence. Jesus' parables and his life of nonviolence invite our commitment to a thoroughgoing agenda of nonviolence. Yet, instead of committing to quality education for the marginalized, affordable housing for the poor, and jobs and mentoring for the young and vulnerable, our nation turns its back when the NRA lobbies, when states build more prisons for people of color and reinstitute and celebrate capital punishment (despite no data to demonstrate that this form of state sanctioned murder curtails crime), war is waged, and the 1972 Anti-Ballistic Missile Treaty discarded. Where is the biblically informed voice of United Methodism that addresses such heinous idolatry and wanton sinfulness? I dissent from our comfortable silence.

The violence in this nation and world provides a grand opportunity for Christians to espouse a different way. A way demonstrated by Jesus whose lifestyle was the radical notion of forgiveness of enemies and love, reconciliation, and receptive hospitality for all people.

So then, in the name of the One who cried from the Cross, "Father forgive them . . .," I affirm a different way. One that refrains from war and employs diplomacy, international sanctions, and United Nations established processes for justice; that dramatically limits gun sales, eliminates capital punishment, slashes the U.S. military budget, replaces the present penchant for prison construction with quality education, and dares to declare a sustained war on poverty with a commitment to jobs, affordable housing, accessible health care, and a serious attack on HIV/AIDS in this nation and around the world. The only underfunded war in this nation's history was the aborted War on Poverty, which could have succeeded if it had enjoyed bipartisan support over the long haul. The abandonment of this necessary war contributed to a lingering despair apparent in many parts of our society today.

I believe it is undebatable that a humane church and national agenda is reflective of the heart of Jesus. But debate it I would with any neoliteralist whose nonbiblical Jesus calls for vengeance, militarism, and the availability of the weapons of violence for begetting more violence, while we affluent Christians pretend war is just and turn our backs on people of color, the poor, and the dispossessed. I cannot find credence for violence and the taking of life, state sanctioned or otherwise, anywhere in the church's memory of Jesus or in the formative years of the early church. I affirm Jesus as Savior, Liberator, and Model. I wonder why we have lost the memory of the early church's pacifism and our Teacher's commitment to lay down everything for the least, last, and lost.

Women

To begin to glimpse the role and place of women in the company of Jesus, one should read Luke—the most universal of the Gospels. Luke intentionally tells his story of Jesus with a profound appreciation for women. In Luke you will find wiser women than were the Magi in Matthew—from Elizabeth and Mary, to Anna in the Temple, to the place of Ruth in the genealogy, to the hospitable woman who dried Jesus' feet with her hair; then to Mary Magdalene, Joanna, and Susanna, who accompanied him on his journey; to Martha and Mary; to the formerly crippled woman whom Jesus healed; to the parabolic floor-sweeper looking for the lost coin; to the tenacious widow before the judge; to the widow with two copper coins; and finally, to Mary Magdalene, Joanna, and Mary the Mother of James at the tomb. Wise and powerful women play a prominent role with Jesus in Luke's account of the gospel.

This is no accident. The radical hospitality of Jesus and the kingdom/reign he initiated were all-inclusive. No one was left behind. There was a place of equality for all—even for women in that patriarchal era in which women were assumed to be property and second-class humans at best.

Much of the Bible reflects a patriarchal bias because of the male-dominated era in which it was written and canonized. As George Orwell reminds us in *1984:* "He who controls the present controls the past. He who controls the past controls the future." This is true with the Bible, church, and most images of God, including the reference to God as Father. This is symbolic language from a male-dominated time and culture. The strong tilt toward the male bias in God language and the leadership stories of the Bible are not exhaustive truth about God and the faithful per se, but a time-bound reflection of a period in history when political and religious power, including that of communication, was of, by, and for men. Males controlled the present, past, and future. Therefore, that women play so prominent a role in the Jesus story in general and in Luke in particular is an indication of the universal radicalism of Jesus. I affirm that women always have been at the Jesus Table. Retreat to the words of 1 Timothy as sacred Truth (words written not by Paul but by an anonymous veteran leader of the early church in the second century) is nonsensical.

Both male-dominated images for God and ecclesiastical assertions that only men should be ordained because the Twelve were men, are context-driven, dated, and biased presentations. They are not definitive of the life of Jesus or the realities of the earliest days of the Christian movement. Therefore, I rejoice in the use of gender inclusive images for God and in the growing presence of women in leadership at all levels of our denomination. In fact, I cannot imagine what would have happened to the quality level among

United Methodist clergy in the last twenty-five years had it not been for the significant influx of many competent women. I affirm the presence of women at the Table and dissent from those who would exclude women by any false and self-serving appeal to scripture or tradition.

I find it curious that many neoliteralists are now embracing women as church leaders despite the words of 1 Timothy. I understand the hermeneutical methodology that inform progressives, but what hermeneutical methodology has moved the neoliteralists from where they were to where they are now? Have the words in the Bible changed? Or are neoliteralists reading and interpreting a portion of the Bible contextually? If so, on this important issue, why not on other subjects?

The Bible simply does not belong only to those who identify themselves as "biblical Christians." The Bible is the sourcebook for the whole Christian community. Many of us, who are not neoliteralists, affirm the Bible as the inspired work of a profoundly faithful, but quite human, community. Actually, the Bible was written by fallible human beings after decades, if not centuries, of oral tradition in response to God's actions in their midst. They wrote in certain historical settings while employing then known theological concepts and available literary devices. They wrote in response to the mystery and majesty of the God who had called them into covenant, made them a people, and personified it all in Jesus. The Bible is not static truth to be lifted out of context, but a living, breathing document the reading, interpreting, and application of which require Spirit empowerment, textual exegesis and exposition, and hard-won conciliar understanding in Christian community. The Bible simply is not the literal Word of God. Such an assertion is idolatry. Jesus, the Risen Christ, is the Word, alive and present in the world. The words and witness of the Bible point to the Christ and to God's antecedent and subsequent revelations of Truth. The Bible is far too important to be taken literally. Rather, the Bible must be taken seriously by a faithful church that employs its best available scholarship, deepest piety and most resolute discipleship that, together, we can hear what the Spirit is saying to us.

I joyfully affirm the primacy of Scripture. I vigorously dissent from the misuse of its wondrous witness.

Conclusion

This chapter is blunt. I am convinced that neoliteralism is idolatry. This powerful movement within today's church, prompted by the uncertainties that plague all of us at a time when everything seems to be coming loose at the seams, has made the words of the Bible the Word. This false approach to the biblical witness has made the Bible an end instead of a means. Yet, neoliteralism is not consistent. I know of no neoliteralist who advocates slavery, polygamy, or infanticide despite biblical words supportive of these practices. Rather, neoliteralists pick and choose biblical passages to suit their own needs.

I affirm the Bible as the primary means whereby God reveals both immanence and transcendence and calls the church and each of us into relationship with the God revealed in Jesus. The primacy of scripture is certain. How we approach this treasure is crucial. I believe that neoliteralism is theologically inconsistent and hurtful to the long-term faithfulness and viability of the whole church. I appeal to progressives to advocate for their understanding of biblical authority in order that the Bible might be rescued from neoliteralism for the benefit of the whole church.

Chapter Four

Fully Human Jesus

Next to biblical authority, Christology, or words about the nature and person of Jesus the Christ, is the second most divisive issue in today's church generally, and within United Methodism specifically.

Rather than probe this core belief of the Christian movement by discussing the pre-Easter Jesus and the post-Easter Christ, the Jesus of history and the Christ of faith, as many scholars have done in quite helpful ways, I shall seek to confess as candidly and vulnerably as I can, who Jesus the Risen Christ is for me.

What follows will offend some. Offense is neither my intent nor purpose. Rather, my hope is to encourage confused believers and those who want to embrace Jesus, but find little meaning in the stilted christological language of the ancient creeds.

Previously, such efforts have brought written complaints of heresy from a few neoliteralists, persons who fail to understand the symbolic nature of religious language. Neoliteralists do not accept the progressive presupposition that words describing matters of ultimate truth are by necessity primarily metaphorical.

I can affirm the orthodox language of the ancient creeds regarding Jesus because I understand, at least in part, the symbolic nature of such religious, theological language. I affirm that Jesus was fully human and fully divine, very God of very God, begotten not made in that he was different, not in substance from other humans, but qualitatively different in his relationship of ultimate trust and absolute obedience to the Holy One he called Abba. I do affirm my faith through the symbolic language, the theological-poetic utterances of the ancient creeds. But it is incumbent upon me as believer and evangelist to unpack this ancient, obtuse language about Jesus in order to make a semblance of finite sense out of infinite mystery on behalf of those who find the ancient creedal language confusing or implausible.

This is not an elitist or academic exercise. There are many thoughtful seekers looking to the church for help with a gnawing spiritual hunger in their hearts. We must open windows to help such people to see the essence of the One whose life, death, and resurrection are the substance of the faith once delivered to the apostles. Anything less is either cowardice or laziness. Thus, for weal or woe, here is who Jesus the Christ is for me.

To state it unequivocally: Jesus was *in toto* fully human. His life was no masquerade. He was the child of human parents, complete with belly button and genetic code. Otherwise, he could not be Liberator, let alone Savior. The Gospel writers provide little in the way of detailed biographical data about Jesus. This is understandable since they were writing theology (Christology in particular) and not history. Their mission was to solidify the church and evangelize others. They wrote accounts that would invite people to listen, believe, and follow, not biographies of Jesus. The four Gospel accounts vary in the person they present, although the three Synoptic (meaning similar stories) Gospels—Matthew, Mark, and Luke—present a composite picture of an itinerant preacher, teacher, and healer who proclaimed and incarnated the reality that in and through him a new age had dawned. This age is the kingdom or reign of God, long awaited by Israel's faithful.

Jesus' primary message was of the present and future reality of this kingdom/reign of God. In it the prophetic hopes and dreams of Israel were being realized as the poor received good news; the blind saw; the lame walked; captives were released from every form of bondage; and believers became new people, transformed disciples like Zacchaeus, Mary Magdalene, Simon Peter, the woman of Samaria, and a host of others.

It is irrefutable, as one searches the Gospel accounts, that Jesus was convinced that the new age of the kingdom/reign had dawned and that his mission was to proclaim it, incarnate it, and invite others into it. For this vision, anchored by his trust in and radical obedience to God, Jesus was crucified, died and was raised.

To assist him in his mission Jesus called a core group of followers, including the inner circle of twelve who were symbolic of the twelve tribes of Israel. Jesus and his followers lived as a covenant community symbolizing the new Israel, a continuation and fulfillment of God's promise to Abraham and Sarah. While the Twelve were at the heart of this new community, many others, including innumerable women, were experiencing the excitement pointing to a new age. But Mark's account of the gospel, in particular, and the other Synoptics, in general, do not hide the reality that the community, especially the Twelve, did not know who Jesus was or what he initiated until after his death and the emerging church's experience of his resurrected presence in their midst. The disciples simply did not get it when Jesus physically was present. Rather, it was only as they "saw" in faith the Risen One that they came to understand, trust, and follow in his steps.

I have chosen not to deal here with John's account of the gospel since it is a later document, which is more attentive to the needs of a developing church late in the first or early in the second century, than to the person and actual ministry of Jesus. Compare John's great "I am" sayings with the parables of the Synoptics. Jesus simply did not preach, teach, or describe himself as John suggests. Rather, John, working in the midst of theological controversies arising in the early church as oppression mounted and dissension developed, took the stories of Jesus, including the witness of the Synoptics, and crafted his particular evangelistic offering for his community in his time and place.

The earlier Synoptic Gospels were written in similar fashion. Each was crafted theologically, with a distinct literary style for a certain audience, as each author employed oral and written sources both common to all three and unique at least to Matthew and Luke. Each Gospel account presents a contextually relevant, theologically informed, evangelistic witness for a particular group or congregation of believers. Nevertheless, despite each evangelist's unique offering, the composite picture of Jesus that emerges from the Synoptics is that of a parabolic teacher, a charismatic preacher, an insightful prophet who was anchored in the covenant of God with Israel, and a healer of possessed souls and broken bodies whose words and deeds were in total congruence with one another.

The complete manifestation of Jesus was claimed by the church after his death and resurrection as the fulfillment of Israel's hopes and dreams and the dawning of the new age. Jesus was affirmed as the expected Messiah, the Christ of God. I believe that Jesus the Messiah, the Christ of God, was fully human. The myth of the Virgin Birth (a theological myth is not a false presentation but a valid and quite persuasive literary device employed to point to ultimate truth that can only be insinuated symbolically and never depicted exhaustively) is found neither in Mark, the earliest Gospel account, nor in John, the latest. This powerful myth was not intended as historical fact, but was employed by Matthew and Luke in different ways to point poetically to the truth about Jesus as experienced in the emerging church. The church believed that Jesus was the long-expected Messiah, the Christ of God, whose revelation was unique and normative. Said differently, in Jesus God's Essence found confluence with a human being and the kingdom/reign was incarnated and ushered into being. The theological myth of the Virgin Birth points to this wondrous mystery and ultimate truth. To treat this myth as a historical fact is to do an injustice to its intended purpose and to run the risk of idolatry, namely, treating a means as an end itself. Thus, if the Virgin Birth did not occur in a physical historical sense, if Jesus were born of human parents, as I affirm he was, and if Jesus did not possess trans-human supernatural powers, as I do not believe he did, what sense can we make of the miraculous stories about him in the Gospel accounts? It is my intent to be candid and vulnerable in responding to these fundamental queries.

God is not a Supreme Being "out there" in the great beyond. Rather, the word *God* is the sound image we humans employ to point to the very Essence of it all that is both in our midst and yet beyond the boundaries of time and existence. Symbolically, if we employ the spatial metaphor developed by Paul Tillich, God is not a Being "out there" or "up there," but the foundation or Ground of all Being. Not limited by time or space, history, or creation, God has been, is, and ever shall be. God is the Essence of it all and is constantly (preveniently, as John Wesley said) at work creating, loving, doing justice, calling humans and all creation into relationship by forgiving, reconciling, empowering, and transforming so that all human beings and the whole created order might be saved. God, as Ground of Being, never quits being God and does not cease from revealing the Essence of it all.

Given this all too brief confession of who and what God is and is not, it follows that Jesus the Christ, in his full humanity did so trust and follow this loving Essence he called "Abba," that he committed himself unequivocally to doing God's will in words and deeds, body, mind, and soul. Jesus in his humanity could have done otherwise. He could have said no to God, but the confluence of God's grace with the human response of faith, as trust and obedience, found perfection in Jesus and the Christ was made manifest. Jesus was not born the Christ. Rather, by the confluence of grace with faith he became the Christ, God's beloved in whom God was well pleased. It was in Jesus' total at-one-ness with God, made possible by God's initiatory actions and Jesus' unequivocably faithful response, that Jesus revealed the heart, the very Essence, of God. When the Gospel writers wrote they sought to portray not merely Jesus of Nazareth but the Christ of God who was alive in their midst.

When the faith community remembered Jesus, they celebrated his resurrected presence in their midst through the breaking of bread, prayer, preaching, teaching, the gift of water, and other means of grace. The church came to confess Jesus not only as the human son of Mary and Joseph, but also as the unique Son of God, the political heir of David, the apocalyptic Son of Man, and the fulfillment of all the hopeful prophecies from Israel's exile and diaspora. From such understandings, Jesus was portrayed as Bethlehem born, the Virgin's child, the long-expected Messiah born to set his people free and, therefore increasingly, as time passed, as the only Son uniquely endowed with those transhuman qualities assumed to be of God. More and more was said about Jesus as the Son of God after his death on the cross as the confused and frightened disciples, who had not gotten it, experienced the Risen Christ in their midst. Profoundly, they got it at last, so they sought appropriate means to tell the story of his unique presence that had transformed their lives and brought the church into being.

Interestingly, Peter, the symbol-person for the whole faith community, could not walk very far on the Sea in Jesus' actual physical presence. But he became so Spirit-filled, so Christ-Essence permeated, on and after the Day of Pentecost, that he became the titular head of the emerging church (leadership he first shared with James and later with Paul). It was Peter who led the church onto and across the sea, that is, into the world of discipleship. It was from their experience of the risen and ever-present Christ Spirit, God's powerful breath of life, that the apostles and disciples came to see through their own trust and obedience that Jesus was not dead and buried but alive forevermore, calling them to pick up his mantle, even to take up the Cross and follow him.

Having said this much, I must say more. I believe in the resurrection of Jesus, but I cannot affirm that his resurrection involved the resuscitation of his physical body. The inconsistent reports in the New Testament of his several and initially unrecognized resurrection appearances add support to this point of view.

A personal experience may help to illustrate. While the innocent, fragile body of our infant son, Mark, was not resuscitated when he died unfairly and far too young from spinal meningitis, I believe, nevertheless, that he and the Risen Christ abide together. The Essence of God, the eternal Spirit of life that flowed completely in and through Jesus and abides from everlasting to everlasting, holds Mark, and all the little children of all ages. This is the same resurrected Jesus power or Christ Essence that infused the disciples and apostles, called the church into being, makes the wounded whole, forgives sin, reconciles and renews, guides history toward justice, drives creation's evolution, and is the foundation of the new age that both is and is to come.

I affirm resurrection, the resurrection of Jesus. God's

Essence cannot be killed, buried, or kept from being active in creation and history. God is from everlasting to everlasting. But, resurrection, including that of Jesus, does not occur through bodily resuscitation. God does not work this way. The issue is not the absence of God's power but God's own "self"-limiting role of revelation in history. God works within the boundaries God has established. And while I do not pretend to know the limits of these boundaries and realize that we all see but through a glass darkly, I am certain that the miracle of resurrection, preeminently that of Jesus, is not tied to bodily resuscitation. The linking of resurrection with bodily resuscitation is to make a literal religious proposition of a metaphorical, symbolic expression of truth itself. This is the kind of idolatry from which I dissent.

I affirm that by God's graceful actions, in confluence with the response of radical obedience and ultimate trust by Jesus, God was uniquely and normatively revealed in Jesus of Nazareth, the Christ of God. And we who do so believe are mandated to follow in the way of Jesus. We are to grow toward perfection by the confluence of divine grace with human faith, as modeled uniquely in the person of Jesus. We are called to be like Jesus in his at-one-ment with God, just as God is gracefully active in us personally and among us as the church. God is calling us to that personal and collective perfection which signals to the world the presence of God's kingdom/reign on earth as it is in heaven.

Having so affirmed Jesus as God's unique and normative revelation, I must dissent from Christocentric exclusivism, which holds that Jesus is the only way to God's gift of salvation. Such an arrogant claim stands over and against the inclusive Jesus of the Synoptics and limits God in ways that humans cannot. God is God, and all human knowledge of that One is limited at best. The Jesus revelation is primary for Christians, and, while I affirm the Christ event as normative, I cannot honestly limit God's ability to be God through revelatory offerings of the Spirit as found in other religions. After all, God's life-giving Spirit found expression in Israel, and the Jews continue to be people of the Covenant. They too are pilgrims on the way. So, too is this the case with God's grace for the faithful followers of Islam. Frankly, I am much more concerned with living out of Jesus' revelation in my life and that of the church than with castigating other religions as being inferior and outside God's eternal plan for salvation. Evangelism is living the good news of Jesus and proclaiming in words and deeds that in Jesus we Christians see and know God. Our personal and communal lives will give credence, or lack thereof, to our witness and call others to—or repel them from—the Jesus way, which I believe is normative, but not the only way to salvation. The other ways may be more circuitous, bumpy, but I trust God to call the family home by whatever means. In the end this mysterious will of God prevails!

I affirm Jesus, the fully human one, as the Son of God, whose relationship of faithful trust and radical obedience with God gave to the church (and through the church to the world) the preeminent manifestation of at-one-ment with God. Atonement is the English contraction for at-one-ment. Obviously, such an understanding of atonement leaves no room for me to affirm the substitutionary atonement theory that portrays Jesus' blood on the cross as satisfying an angry deity through one majestic sacrificial human death, much as sacrifices of unblemished sheep and goats in ancient Israel were understood to appease God and atone for the sins of all.

Sacrifice, even of one's life, on behalf of others is an eloquent witness to God's grace. Jesus died for others, doubtlessly. Nevertheless, I find the substitutionary atonement theory, which is but one of several Christian theories of atonement, to be at odds with other images of God reflected by the witness of Jesus and experienced by this writer. In fact, I am convinced that quite often such unexamined thought repels many intelligent, sensitive, searching people and drives some of them from understanding, accepting, and following the God revealed in Jesus, who is the One for whom their aching hearts yearn. How much more blood sacrifice is needed in a world saturated with blood and famished for a different understanding of salvation? While sacrifice as an act of discipleship is essential for all of us as it was for Jesus, the concept of blood sacrifice to appease God is superstition at best and an idolatrous allegiance to a non-Jesus methodology of God-human relationship at worst. Historically and presently, the church has other models of atonement theory to offer a hurting world. The time has come for progressives courageously to claim the atonement of Jesus as that which is reflective of everything he did and all he was, namely, the One who was in such at-one-ness with God that he could suffer and die for others.

To understand Jesus' at-one-ment with God as the confluence of God's grace with Jesus' radical obedience and complete trust that thus manifests the kingdom/reign of God which is to be offered in inclusive hospitality by the church to the world, presupposes an evangelistic mission that proclaims that, in Jesus, God has been made manifest among us making eternal life, life with meaning and purpose, available now. I believe that the gift of eternal life, as relationship of at-one-ment with God, continues after death and that we Christians are to live and witness here and now in such ways that God's gift of eternal life is available for all who, being welcomed and coached, accepted and guided, and not judged and cast away by the church, will dare in faith stimulated by grace to say yes to Jesus' way. This way of living is a lifelong process of total reorientation of will and being away from self toward God and for all humankind in a life of internal piety and external unquenchable fire for mission, justice, and evangelism. Undoubtedly, we progressives have been lax in our evangelistic zeal for fear of being misunderstood as proselytizers, or because our trust and obedience have been found wanting. In either case to affirm Jesus as the Christ means that believers commit to living radically obedient and ultimately trusting lives in response to God's grace as we follow Jesus the Christ, who consummated his *at-one-ment* on the Cross. This I affirm. I do dissent from neoliteralist Christology and the failure of progressives to name the name of Jesus. Therefore, I urge neoliteralists to shun idolatry, and progressives to awaken to the evangelistic task and opportunity God in Christ is presenting all of us, for the living of these days.

Conclusion

Jesus was fully human and fully divine. His humanity was given in his conception and birth through the natural processes of procreation. His divinity was derived, given as gift, from his relationship of trust and obedience with God.

The way of Jesus is informative for his disciples. The whole church is called to follow him by responding in trust and obedience to the divine initiative that yearns for relationship with humans and longs to make us aware of our identity as children of God, brothers and sisters of Jesus, and of all humankind.

Chapter Five

Hope Is the Thing

Standing for possible election to the episcopacy at the North Central Jurisdiction Conference in July 1996 and during the early years of my episcopal ministry, I was asked one question more frequently than any other, *What is the most important issue facing the United Methodist Church today?*

My response then, and now: *The near absence of hope, especially among clergy, that creates fear on the right and cynicism on the left. Both of these realities are symptomatic of a deep theological malaise, even that of practical atheism.*

Too many on the right fearfully cling to past certitudes found in a literal reading of creeds and scripture, as if the Spirit were not dynamically alive in our midst opening new understandings and demanding new interpretations. Too many on the left simply react to new challenges by behaving as if God were not at work calling all of us to expanded vistas of faithfulness.

Given my response about hope that has been validated during my tenure as a bishop through innumerable one-on-one conversations, in small group gatherings with clergy, and by hundreds of congregational visits, I am convinced that the essential role of a bishop in these days is to model active hope. This hope must flow from a deep and abiding sense of the reality of God's active presence in the life of the world, church, and the bishop himself or herself. I am convinced that a bishop must model hopeful ministry that flows naturally from his or her own maturing spirituality, intellectual honesty, and day-to-day courageous and risk-taking practice of ministry. This I have tried to do. There are encouraging signs that such embraced hope is making a difference among innumerable clergy and with many congregations in our conference. These signs are evident in the qualitative difference in clergy morale and through tangible indicators of congregational, district, and conference renewal, particularly in increased worship attendance for each of the past five years.

As I have attempted to model hope faithfully, these words of Emily Dickinson have echoed constantly in my soul and from my lips:

> Hope is the thing with feathers,
> That perches in the soul.
> And sings the tune without the words,
> And never stops—at all.

Hope based on the gospel proclamation and anchored in the reality of Jesus' resurrection is that gift of God which the whole church, right, left, and middle, most needs today. I affirm God's hope reflected completely in Jesus the Risen One. I claim it as the basis for faithful, courageous ministry. Thus, I dissent from the fear of the right, the cynicism of the left, and the mediocrity of the middle. All these reactions are tangible reflections of the near absence of gospel hope.

The recovery of gospel hope calls for renewed attention to biblical and theological study, prayer, and small group life, holistic evangelism and risk-taking, hands-on mission, and justice work in the world. Business as usual will not work in today's church. We are in the beginning of the third age of the church, a new apostolic age in which the church is no longer revered and treated as a shaper of the United States culture, but instead increasingly is viewed as separate from, if not alien to, the mainstream. New times demand new methodologies as well as a renewed anchoring in core beliefs and fundamental commitments unique to those who are a part of the Body of Christ.

Speaking platitudes of hope, without embracing strategic, informed, and intentional actions, is mere pious illusion. If we embrace authentic hope that emerges from renewed trust in and commitment to the God who raised Jesus, this reality must take feet and walk. Such hope cannot remain mired in the status quo of fear, cynicism, and staid middle-of-the-road politics that have emerged within the Church in recent years.

I suggest the following as indicators of active and intentional hope.

First, congregations that regularly embrace four essential marks of vitality;

Second, annual conferences that support, encourage, and extend these congregations, while challenging those that are not vital;

Third, general church agencies that cease being fiefdoms of personal power and, instead, become brokers of opportunity and empowerment;

And fourth, bishops and a Council of Bishops that will dare to lead with courage and resolute commitment, trusting that unity is the gift God gives and not a fragile commodity bishops are to preserve.

Vital congregations, regardless of size or setting, exhibit at least these four essential marks of vitality:

(1) *Passionate worship* that is both blended and of several diverse styles, but always biblically centered with faithful preaching, soulful music, and active sacramental practices at its heart.

(2) *Sophisticated education* for adults (youth and children's ministries are presupposed in today's Church in that they are non-negotiable if vitality is to exist) that enlists the

pastor as a primary teacher with adults through weekly lectionary study, Disciple Bible Study, short-term courses on United Methodism and the Social Principles, seminary-level offerings of the works of the theological giants of our time, as well as of the great reformers, mystics, and saints of the earlier church, and such other courses as are contextually relevant. I urge our conference pastors to lead at least three adult groups/classes per week. My experience is that the adults who are returning or coming to the church for the first time hunger, not for theological pablum, but for the solid food of our best thinking, especially in theology and biblical studies.

(3) *Intimate care groups* that enable every willing adult to belong to a small group in which she or he can learn to pray and to know and be known by others. Our souls long for intimate antidotes to the loneliness and anonymity of modern life. Small groups provide such a response and are at the heart of congregational renewal. Nurturing programs like Covenant Discipleship, Christian Believer, and Disciples of Christ in Community are marvelous offerings for any size congregation.

(4) *Risk-taking, wholistic, hands-on mission, social justice, and evangelism* regularly practiced and expected in order that busy people be provided, weekly as well as seasonally, conduits through which to make a difference with and for others. All maturing Christians long to have their lives count for Christ and with others. Volunteers in Mission, Shalom, and Congregation Based Organizing are powerful tools that vital congregations can embrace lest attempts at renewal become parochial, in-grown, and a new brand of navel-gazing and self-preoccupation.

The key to congregational revitalization is clergy leadership. Pastors who are so called by God, trained in seminary, and supported by laity, bishops, and district superintendents that they will dare to color outside the lines. I ask our clergy to spend 50 percent of their time preparing for and doing the essential work of teaching, preaching, and leading worship. If this is done, faithfully and well, all else will follow. God is thereby provided open access to congregations and the world in order to do the work of the kingdom/reign.

Annual conferences are not parachurch entities unto themselves, but a part of the whole. They are the key links that connect congregation to congregation, clergy to clergy, and all to the whole church in mission to the world. Fundamentally, annual conferences are conduits for recruiting, equipping, and sending leaders, both clergy and lay, and for gathering the necessary financial resources to extend justice, mission, and evangelism to the wider reaches of nation and globe. Annual conferences must be resource centers filled with ideas, experts, helpers, and guides who will coach congregations in processes of revitalization and help extend them as outposts for mission, evangelism, and justice doing. Sessions of the annual conference should be grand occasions for celebration. These celebrations must be steeped in passionate, soul-stirring worship. Time must be provided for storytelling especially regarding what is happening and can happen in vital, diverse congregations of all sizes in every locale.

We have fooled ourselves by thinking that, if our own political or theological position is endorsed by a resolution at annual conference, we have been faithful and addressed the issue at hand. If judicatory resolutions could save the world, the kingdom/reign would be here in full glory. Issues of life and death are addressed daily in the ebb and flow of faithful ministry especially by the laity who labor in the trenches of the world. The sessions of annual conference, instead of being strident occasions for caucus groups to engage in grandiose infighting, must become sacred moments for rejoicing, learning, planning, recommitting, and being empowered to act on all that God requires and makes possible in the year ahead. I am beginning to glimpse the possibility that sessions of many annual conferences will be so passionate, rich, and invaluable that they will produce sustaining memories for all the hard days and tough nights that lie ahead. I harbor an expectation, based on what is being done across the connection, that such sessions are becoming a possibility. I affirm this dream.

I cannot fathom a denomination such as United Methodism without general program agencies. We are too big and have too much to do to function without them. But we no longer have the luxury of duplications of effort and turf battles that for too long have characterized general agency life. These struggles, often the raw stuff of power politics, occasionally preclude, sometimes water down, and nearly always stall getting necessary resources of money and personnel to places of dire need and pregnant possibility. Such behavior cannot be tolerated any longer. I dissent from our seeming unwillingness to address this festering sore.

The General Council on Ministries could very well seize this moment in time, assume its authority, and coordinate hard-nosed cooperative efforts to eliminate senseless duplications among the agencies. For example, they might examine how many pockets there are in various agencies to which ethnic congregation must go to seek grants for crying needs in tough arenas for ministry. I dissent from this unnecessary misuse of congregational and pastoral time and effort. There is no excuse for us, as well-organized, well-intended and well-disciplined United Methodists, to allow vast reserves of money and personnel to lie fallow when children are dying, hearts are aching for the gospel, churches need to be built, pastors need to be trained, and various isms of this world must be eradicated. I cannot accept quietly what I have seen in Third World mission sites where too often United Methodism is unable to get to those outposts of God's hope all that is needed for effective ministry in timely fashion. We must stop making excuses and start doing that which hope dictates and faith demands.

The bishops of our denomination are admirable people. They are deeply committed disciples and gifted clergy who have been elected to provide leadership for the Church and world. But occasionally, in our Areas and nearly always in the Council of Bishops, we bishops are reticent to pick up the mantle of leadership, granted by election and confirmed in consecration, to lead the Church with the kind of vision and courage God demands and those who elected us rightfully expect. We bishops have allowed ourselves to be victimized by fear and cynicism. Fear of what our critics will say or charge. Fear that we are doing program work when that is not our role. Fear that the Judicial Council will embarrass us with yet another rigid verdict and more harsh words. Fear that we will be misunderstood and that our people will be upset. And, cynical that the episcopacy has become superfluous and that we are irrelevant relics from the pre-megachurch days. I dissent from our fears and cynicism. They are manifestations of hopelessness that are rendering the Council of Bishops powerless to lead.

The question facing those of us who are bishops is what to do with the mantle of leadership we have been called upon to wear. Will we lead or won't we? I shudder with ecstasy when I envision the kind of energy and hope that would be unleashed in the Church if the Council of Bishops were to say what it really believes, point the Church where we perceive it must go, and dare not only to stand with others, but also to say, "Over here. Over here. God in Christ is calling the Church to be bold—bolder than we have ever been."

Some may assume that I am talking primarily about

social issues, especially peace, sexuality, poverty, and race. I am. But I am also talking about holistic evangelism; the fallacy of guaranteed appointments; the needed renewal of itineracy; the longing for contextual, well-funded seminary education; congregational development and redevelopment; and the mandate for our collective voice to be raised with authoritative solidarity on matters of marriage and the family, drugs, HIV/AIDS, immigration, bioethics, ecology, and the exploitation of the vulnerable by a United States culture of materialistic consumerism. I am convinced that we bishops are becoming so paralyzed by fear and cynicism that in our attempts to please everybody we often fail to exert the kind of theological, pastoral, and prophetic leadership Jesus modeled and calls us to emulate. Some of my most respected Church colleagues are bishops; it is our collective reticence I find intolerable. Thus, while I affirm my colleagues in the Council of Bishops as valued brothers and sisters in Christ, I dissent from our collective fear and cynicism, of which I am a part.

United Methodism does not need megachurch pundits, demographic gurus, or slick marketing experts to accomplish the renewal and revitalization all of us crave and believe that God is eager to bestow upon the Church we love. Rather, solid biblical and theological hope is what is needed among clergy and congregations, in annual conferences and general agencies, within my soul, and among all of us in the Council of Bishops. Strategies will follow, as a wagon follows a team of pulling horses, if only we can sing from the heart, "Hope is the thing. . . ."

Conclusion

Biblical hope is anchored in the God of the Covenant who always makes a way where there seems to be no way. This God is our only absolute.

This reality was evident in the Exodus and is preeminently reflected in the resurrection of Jesus. The evil that killed him and the arrogance that entombed him seemingly won the day. But we believe that his day of death was *Good* Friday because God used the Cross and empty tomb to proclaim vividly who the Victor is. To believe this fundamental affirmation means that our hope is anchored in God who appropriates faithful discipleship, sometimes against great odds, to raise up new possibilities. The victory of nonviolence in the Civil Rights movement, the fall of the Berlin Wall, and the end of apartheid in South Africa bear vivid witness to this reality.

This story is told of a small Protestant church in East Germany that had suffered terribly during Communist rule. When the Wall fell, the pastor wrote these words on the small sign in front of the church building, "The Lamb Wins!"

I affirm that Christian hope is not humanistic optimism but trust in the God of the Exodus who raised Jesus and will bring to actuality the kingdom/reign Jesus initiated whenever the people of God are found faithfully living lives of committed discipleship. Such lives take their cue, not from the culture, but from the presence of the Risen Christ who is alive and well.

Hope is the thing that is essential for us.

Chapter Six

Leadership, Leadership, Leadership

"If the loss of hope is the primary issue facing our Church today, what is the second most important matter we must address?" "Leadership, leadership, leadership" has been and remains my reply to this recurring question.

Next to the necessity of hope's recovery, the recruitment, training, nurture, and support of dynamic, creative, and courageous leadership is the most important issue facing the United Methodist Church. This need for a new generation of leaders begins with the clergy.

Needed: Clergy who are called by God into ordained ministry. Clergy with theologically grounded commitments to loving-kindness, doing justice, and walking humbly with God and a diverse, inclusive community of sisters and brothers. And clergy with the courage of their commitments and the willingness to stand for them in congregations, annual conferences, the general church, and the world.

The Church today does not need chancel prancers who debate the virtues of the various venues of worship—contemporary or traditional, formal or informal. We need faithful preachers who dare to be so anchored in scripture and theology and so conversant with the yearnings of human hearts that, stretched between essence and existence, emotionally and theologically vulnerable but not ashamed, the Word of God will flow authentically from their well-crafted words and vulnerable lives.

The Church today does not need organizational development gurus who major in process, but fail to help produce converted lives and transformed communities. We need courageous and visionary leaders who so trust the presence of the Spirit that they will dare to say, "Over here, over here, God is calling us to mission and witness over here."

The Church today does not need technological wizards who spend countless hours hiding behind the latest technology. Technology is a tremendous tool, a gifted means, for the end of doing ministry. But it must not be treated as an end, as too many clergy do. We need well-informed teachers who will spend their lives in the midst of searching groups of laity so that a biblically and theologically hungry Church will once again be fed the feasts of faith, hope, love, justice, courage, sacrifice, and mercy contained in the biblical witness.

The Church today does not need passive pray-ers who are content to be bookends at civic functions, praying little invocations and tiny benedictions—innocuous prayers of civic piety that bless the status quo. We need highly participatory prophets who, through Congregation Based Organizing and Communities of Shalom, will dare to help shape a new agenda for Church and world.

The Church today does not need timid practitioners of institutional mediocrity who walk on eggs and break none in order to gain ascendancy in the clergy club. We need courageous egg breakers who dare to scramble and fluff new omelettes of risk-taking mission, passionate worship, intimate community care, sophisticated education, holistic evangelism, and systemic social change.

The Church today does not need either additional cynics on the left, more fear peddlers on the right, or placid pleasers in the center—we have a plethora of all of these. We need clergy of resilient hope, who know with the poet that "Hope is the thing." Not needed today are more professional parasites who are content to feed on the institutional carcass, which has been picked almost bare. We need a new breed of clergy who dare to believe that God has called them for such a pregnant time as this to spread scriptural holiness around the globe, while recalling John Wesley's admonition that there is no holiness but social holiness.

I affirm that God is calling such ordained clergy into ministry and leadership. I am thankful that a growing number of such faithful and effective priestly and prophetic pastors are emerging in our midst. The fact is that wherever such leaders are appointed, regardless of context or ethnicity, in town and rural settings, new church starts, core city parishes or affluent suburban congregations, wondrous things are happening. I affirm the need for leadership, leadership, leadership.

But, these deeply committed, highly creative and discernibly courageous clergy are too few and too far between. This is not because God has not and is not calling needed leaders to ordained ministry but because, too often, the Church and we who lead it have been negligent in inviting those called to enter ordained ministry.

Therefore, I dissent from:

(1) *Clergy shame that has so enslaved some clergy that they are embarrassed to invite others into ordained ministry.* Shame that is enhanced by a culture that does not lavishly reward faithfulness in ministry. Shame that immobilizes clergy who do not have sufficient spiritual moorings to find satisfaction and meaning internally when external prestige and power are not abundant.

(2) *An outdated seminary system that shuns contextual education and puts too much money into too many isolated academic institutions and not enough into student and faculty support.* We need student-friendly contextual education that takes

theological training into the various settings where students live and minister. We simply must create a funding plan that defrays the astronomical costs of a seminary education in today's world, if we are to attract and keep the vast number of exceptional leaders needed. Here technology could serve us well if we developed many avenues for "distant learning" by the Internet as one of the means for offering contextual education.

(3) *Our historic but quiet embrace of mediocrity in the promotion of clergy.* Instead of putting talent and commitment where they are needed, we have too often protected the mediocre and rewarded those who neither upset anyone nor led the Church to make a difference in lives and communities. We can no longer hide and protect unwilling or unable clergy in our midst. The itinerant system, with its promise of guaranteed appointments, while caring for women and clergy of color in ways the call system cannot and does not, needs systemic attention. This includes eliminating the practice of guaranteed appointments that forces bishops to continue to appoint clergy we know cannot or will not provide the leadership needed for the Church today. Most cabinets spend 90 percent of their time dealing with 10 percent of the clergy.

(4) *The failure of high-profile veteran clergy, including bishops, to mentor and provide authentic replicable models of courageous and effective leadership for today's younger clergy to emulate.* Despite these serious dissents, I do affirm what God is doing in our midst in continuing to call able women and men into ordained ministry. I affirm the mentoring and modeling work that is beginning to emerge in the whole Church. All is not lost, not by a long shot.

Given our leadership needs and God's call, I offer the following suggestions for the Church to debate, adapt, and adopt.

First, we must recommit to the training and support of a

new generation of campus and youth pastors who will work with an emerging youth and student movement to prepare young people for the abundant leadership opportunities awaiting them.

Second, we should encourage congregations, districts and annual conferences to establish summer intern programs in congregational settings for older teens who sense that God just might be "messing with their lives." Let teens shadow our most able clergy and learn to do by doing, while catching the excitement of living in response to God's wondrous call to discipleship through the practice of ordained ministry.

Third, we need to forgo the luxury of embracing uncritically the latest "how to grow" fads and, instead, train a new generation of clergy in the fundamentals of the Christian faith. Clergy must be taught biblical studies, theology, church history, and how to preach, teach, organize, and empower congregations. Congregations and veteran clergy can help if the academy will ask. Together, we can establish new contexts in the midst of congregational and community life for the training of clergy.

Fourth, the ministries of teaching and preaching must become primary foci among the ordained. I am convinced that every ordained deacon and elder should be leading at least three groups or classes a week. Remember, we are aliens in a culture that could care less about us. We must know who and whose we are. It is absolutely essential that we know the stories that convey the Story, that we can trace the pictures in the family album that is the Bible, and that we can describe how those lives have fused to form the mosaic of all the saints on whose shoulders we stand.

This teaching ministry begins with the biblical witness. It is time for the ordained to take off the protective gloves, roll up our sleeves, and get our hands dirty as we dare to share with the laity what we learned in seminary. Now is the opportune time to help laity read and understand the Bible again, often for the first time. Now is the time to empower laity to learn to listen to biblical texts metaphorically and expectantly. Now is the time for all of us to hear anew what the Spirit is saying to us and the whole Church.

How is this accomplished? By leading Disciple Bible Studies. By introducing programs such as Disciples of Christ in Community, Christian Believer, and Covenant Discipleship. By engaging laity, as well as other clergy, in weekly lectionary studies so as to shape sermons in correlation with biblical text and congregational context. By daring to introduce laity to the Social Principles and to the most challenging historic and present-day theological thinking. Laypeople in the Church are hungry not for grade school biblical and theological pablum but for a graduate school feast of the beans and rice, tofu and noodles, meat and potatoes of life-changing and death-defying sophisticated biblical and theological exploration and exposition. Clergy must learn to trust the laity and to lay aside the paralyzing fear that solid theologizing will alienate them. The opposite is true. I affirm the laity as God's ministers in the world. Clergy must help to empower the laity for their discipleship by doing well what we have been ordained to do. I am convinced that bishops and other veteran clergy must model effective teaching and preaching ministries from which others can learn, draw strength, and discover increased resolve for the pursuit of excellence in ordained ministry. Clergy must preach as if our hearts and souls are on fire with the Spirit. I once heard a Quaker evangelist say, "Get on fire for Christ Jesus and folks will gather to watch you burn." Yes! And in the process the sparks will light fires of illumination, purpose, and meaning in them and in others. Many others. It only takes a spark to get a fire going.

I rejoice that we United Methodists have recovered our

sacramental heritage. It is a gift of the ecumenical movement that we have rediscovered the power of the sensual for matters spiritual. Water, Cup, and Bread are rightly central in our worship life. The ordained are privileged beyond words to pour Water, break Bread and elevate the Cup. But as sacramental as our roots may be, and as sacramental as we need to be for such a time as this, sacramental liturgies are no substitute for quality preaching. It is Word and Table, not Table and Word, and surely never Table without Word. We are Protestants and United Methodists at that! Preaching is to our communal ethos as blue is to the sky in the heart of July or as flawed pitching and untimely hitting are to the Chicago Cubs in September. Few good, let alone exceptional, preachers are born that way. Most learn the art of preaching by listening, reading, writing, and praying. Preaching is a labor of love. But it is quite often hard labor.

It has been said: "An hour in the study for each minute in the pulpit." Too extreme for today, most say. In fact, if this were still the operating maxim, United Methodist worship services would be mere sound bites. Supposedly, we have other more important matters to attend to than weekly, disciplined sermon preparation. Matters such as meetings, places to go, computers to punch, an Internet to scan, e-mail to read. I dissent from our poor use of time as clergy.

Granted, even the most disciplined clergy do not have an abundance of time for sermon preparation. Nevertheless, there is no substitute for diligent homiletical work. While there are many valid methodologies for solid homiletical work, I offer the following as a model that has worked for me.

(a) Do biblical exegesis on Monday or Tuesday;

(b) Organize textual and contextual conversations with laity on Wednesday (I call these sessions Sermon Shaping);

(c) Write a manuscript on Thursday;

(d) Pray, listen, imagine, dream, and integrate on Friday and/or Saturday, as you transform the written text into oral form; and,

(e) Come Sunday—and Sunday always comes—consider leaving your written manuscript in the study, whenever possible. When speaking with the congregation, allow the Word to flow as you dare to preach stretched vulnerably between essence and existence.[1]

What a privilege it is to "Preach the Word." What an opportunity this spiritual art form provides for leading the Church and addressing the world. This chapter has devoted many words to teaching and preaching because I believe that clergy should spend half of their working hours preparing for and doing the work of teaching and preaching.

I affirm that God in Christ is seeking to do kingdom/reign of God work in the United Methodist Church. The Spirit's wind is blowing, and it will sweep us to new heights of vitality and renewal if we embrace its power and dare to soar.

Conclusion

Baptism is the sacrament of initiation. Through this means of grace Christians are made part of the family of God, brothers and sisters of Jesus. Baptism makes all recipients ministers, laity and clergy alike.

This chapter presupposes that clergy are ordained for certain functions in order to equip the laity, theologically and biblically, for lives of discipleship in the world.

---

1. This methodology presupposes that one of the days noted will be the preacher's necessary day off. Friday is my customary day off for self-care and pure enjoyment.

Laity helps to validate the faithfulness of the clergy by their faithful ministries of love, justice, mission, and evangelism in the world.

The Church will be renewed as clergy are faithful in our calling to empower the laity. And the Church will be renewed as an empowered laity practices informed and authentic discipleship in the world. Each part is integral to the other, both are essential to the well-being of the whole Church.

Such is the call to each of us for leadership, leadership, leadership.

Chapter Seven

Seamless Garment

Given my formative years and the initial call to ordained ministry in the Teddy Bear Restaurant, I have not been able to separate evangelism from mission, worship and prayer from social justice. To hold the hand of a beloved parishioner, as death did its bidding, was a privileged pastoral act, not unlike advocating for peace and nonviolence or for change in the welfare and education systems, or standing for justice with immigrants and migrant farm workers, or contending with the evils of racism, sexism, or heterosexism.

My theological understanding affirms that pastoral and prophetic acts, priestly functions, and change-oriented administrative practices are inseparable parts of the composite of ordained ministry whether in the congregation, bureaucratic office, or episcopacy. The present line of demarcation some draw in practice, if not in theory, between evangelism and church growth on the one hand and social justice actions on the other is myopic, if not heretical. Ministry is for the world so that individual persons and entire groups of people might be set free to know and live joyfully in the love of God as revealed in Jesus. Strategies for faithful ministry are varied, depending on context. They are always a reflection of the confluence of loving-kindness, doing justice, and walking humbly with God, while acting hospitably with needful people, whether they are allies or adversaries, and working for systemic change for the body politic.

This view and empowering passion suggest that there is a seamless garment which contains within it not only an inherent lifestyle for the practice of ordained ministry, but also a plethora of intertwined issues no one of which can be separated from the other. This includes the issue of peace with justice that 9/11 has forced us to reexamine in the midst of the grief, fear, and anger, if not rage, that permeate the church and culture in this nation. Experiencing the grief and disorientation that are so real among the clergy and within the whole church in the aftermath of terrorist attacks and United States–led counterattacks, I wrote a number of pastoral letters and/or newspaper columns for the Northern Illinois Conference in September, October, and November of 2001.

My September 12, 2001, Pastoral Letter to the whole Conference said in part the following:

> Hearing the news of yesterday's stark tragedy, my heart cried. For a moment, I was parent and nothing else. Our elder son travels a great deal. He went to the World Trade Center often. Was he there when evil exploded? Indescribable relief overwhelmed me when I learned that he was safe in Houston.
>
> But what of countless thousands not so fortunate? How can such unfathomable devastation and indescribable carnage be understood, integrated, accepted? They cannot. At least, not easily and not now.
>
> The scriptures help. "God is our refuge and strength, a very present help in trouble. Therefore, we will not fear, though the earth should change" (Psalm 46:1-2a).
>
> We are the Church. Our trust is in the God as revealed in Jesus. And we have one another in the bonds of Christian community. We can lean on the everlasting arms and embrace one another. From such sources are strength and hope renewed. . . .
>
> *The 2000 United Methodist Book of Resolutions* says, "The image of God and the sacrifice of Christ bestow a worth and

dignity that cannot be rightfully ignored or violated by any human institution or social movement. For this reason, *we condemn all acts of terrorism*" (page 787).

We United Methodists absolutely condemn the heinous acts of terrorism that were perpetrated on Tuesday, September 11, 2001, without regard for the basic tenets of civility and with utter disregard for the sanctity of human life. . . .

Our United Methodism resolution continues: "examine (it asks us) critically the cause of terrorism, including national and international involvement. . . ."

It is time, as we mourn this nation's dead and confront our rage, to move boldly to eliminate the conditions that conceive and give birth to the lunacy that struck yesterday. Monsters are created by monstrous circumstances. God is calling us in the midst of our numbness, fear, and natural instinct to demand eyes for eyes to care for the thousands of innocent victims and their loved ones, to seek justice by appropriate means for the perpetrators, and to urge our government to broker a just and lasting peace. . . .

We must not, as followers of Jesus, wrongly condemn all Muslims for the despicable actions of a crazed fringe. Be not mistaken, such violent fanatics do not adhere to the basic tenets of Islam. It behooves us to set an example of God's intent as we reach out in love to the countless Middle Easterners—Jews, Muslims, and Palestinian Christians—who live faithfully and peacefully among us. . . .

Now is the time for us to recommit ourselves to follow Jesus in all we say and do. Our mission is to walk the talk as we hear Jesus say to us, "Blessed are the merciful, for they will receive mercy. Blessed are the pure in heart, for they will see God. Blessed are the peacemakers, for they will be called children of God" (Matthew 5:7-9).

I followed the Pastoral Letter with this column in the October 5 conference newspaper.

The question, "How could this happen?" is a military, intelligence, or political query in many settings. But, most often, when it is asked in religious circles, it is a theological inquiry. Usually it means, "How could God allow such a tragedy to occur?"

God did not cause this calamity, despite what some have said. God is not some supreme being who resides in the vast beyond looking down on us to make harsh, devastating judgments. God is not a tough male judge who examines the scales of justice and then either rewards or punishes the just and unjust.

Rather, God is the Essence or Ground of all creation and history. God is in the midst of all life, yet independent of it as well. God is the love, power, creativity, and purpose at the heart of it all who never ceases revealing the attributes of divinity. God never ceases yearning for and calling humankind into relationship with the divine. Jesus manifests the joy and power of such relationship, of such at-one-ment of the divine and human.

Humans are created with the capacity, the never-dying need, for relationship with God. To the degree that in faith, which is trust and responsive, courageous, obedience, we respond to God, we reflect God's revelations. When we turn away from God, we both reveal and personify ungodliness, the most diabolical manifestation of which is abject evil. Evil is a reality in the world; it can take root within each of us and among groups of us. It results from turning away from God in unfaith while serving the isms of this world.

Evil's way is made easier when hard circumstances such as oppression, abuse, abject poverty, and ignorance are dominant in a person's or group's experience. Such painful realities make the leap of faith difficult. It is difficult to embrace love and goodness, if you have only known hatred and malevolence.

The choice for evil and not good, for violence and not love, for ungodliness and not relationship with God, whether God is called Yahweh, Allah, or the "Abba" of Jesus, was what made possible the horrific tragedies of September 11.

But before we too quickly cast our understandable rage and total blame only on the perpetrators and those who helped to make possible their heinous deeds, it is incumbent upon us as individual Christians, the Church, and Americans to examine and change all aspects of our behavior—theological, political, economic, military, and cultural—that may have helped to foster the conditions from which such wrong-headed choices for the embrace of evil emerged. Monstrous circumstances produce monstrous deeds.

What can we do? I suggest three things immediately. First, *embrace the pain.* Second, *seize the time.* Third, *extend the discourse.*

Embrace the pain by entering with one another into the grief and rage that are present within and among us. Now is the time for listening and embracing across all lines of separation and division. Henri Nouwen called Christians to transform hostility into hospitality by creating the receptive space of acceptance, in the midst of human differences, in which the Holy Spirit has room to work the miracles of understanding, forgiveness, and healing. It is time to embrace our pain in a context of extended hospitality.

Seize the time to be Church. Now is the time to point to the unconditional love of God—the only absolute in a world of change—as revealed in Jesus. Now is the time for our worship to be spiritually passionate. For our teaching to be biblically and theologically informed. For our communal life to be welcoming, affirming, and prayerful. For our evangelistic, missional, and justice work to focus on a hurting world and broken people yearning for good news. The Church has been created and commissioned to incarnate, proclaim, and give away good news. *Seize the time* to be Church.

Extend the discourse by helping the uninformed to better understand the religion of Islam. Stand, as so many of you have, against any stereotyping of Muslims, Palestinians, Arabs, or Jews. Speak against any disproportionate act or acts of revenge or retaliation. For this nation to kill innocent persons elsewhere, while rightly seeking the perpetrators, will only foster those circumstances from which more hatred and additional terrorists will emerge. Teach that all innocent children, women, and men are of equal value in God's sight. For any to be killed, here or elsewhere, breaks the heart of God and denies the teachings of Jesus. *Extend the discourse* everywhere.

God did not cause the events of September 11. The embrace of evil did. Evil that was given opportunity to extend itself when God's goodness was shunned.

We can and we must be so related to God, through Jesus, that fundamental goodness will be made manifest and given additional opportunities to thrive. In such ways will evil be defeated and God's reign hastened.

God did not cause death to occur but God yearns to make fullness of life possible for all people.

It is our task to be a harbinger—not of death and destruction—but of such life.

Later, following the initiation of Mr. Bush's military phase of his war on terrorism, I wrote the following column on October 19.

Sadness floods my soul.

The personal stories, complete with photographs, of the September 11 victims and their families overwhelm me. So do the media accounts of the Afghan people. Poverty-stricken, politically and socially oppressed, and cowering in fear of United States military firepower, these *anaweim* (the broken little ones of the earth) are caught in a Catch-22. They are damned if they do and damned if they don't.

The fear of children and youth in this nation, like that of their peers around the globe, haunts me. So does the National Public Radio broadcast I heard on the afternoon of October 6. Driving home from distant speaking engagements, I listened to an Iraqi refugee in Canada describe the sheer terror of holding his three-year-old son as they awaited the expected United States missile to end life as they knew it. It was he who described some 5,000 deaths per month of children, women, and men in Iraq because of the blockade of food and medicine since the Gulf War. Saddam Hussein, like bin Laden, is one reality. Innocent people are something else. So I grieve. Sadness weighs heavily with sighs almost too heavy for coherent expression.

Luke 17:5-10, a Gospel lection for World Communion Sunday, contained Jesus' follow-up parables to his teaching about forgiveness. Because he taught and incarnated unlimited forgiveness, the apostles cried, "Increase our faith." Faith is both trust in God's unconditional love and obedience to God's will. Jesus is clear about how faith eventuates in forgiveness and how in faith we are to embrace and practice this fundamental of discipleship.

Forgiveness was a powerful reminder on World Communion Sunday. But the words of forgiveness were shattered as World Communion Sunday services ended and we learned that military operations had begun in Afghanistan. I applaud Mr. Bush's program of food and medical supplies. But I am sad, profoundly so, about the military operation. I fear that more innocent people will be killed. In God's view, all wars are civil wars. We are all part of God's good, if fallen, creation. I am sad because God's heart is wounded by violence. And history clearly teaches that violence begets more violence, always senseless and increasingly horrific.

Our United Methodist position on war is clear and unequivocal. The General Conference in May 2000 said, "We believe war is incompatible with the teachings and example of Christ. We therefore reject war as a usual instrument of national foreign policy and insist that the first moral duty of all nations is to resolve by peaceful means every dispute. . . . Human values must outweigh military claims" (Paragraph 165.C, War and Peace, page 121). But I read the polls. Ninety-three percent of the U.S. citizenry supports military action. Our United Methodist position is that of a miniscule minority. With a sad heart I ask, "How can we be faithful to Jesus, loyal to the Church, and dissenting patriots in the nation we love? . . ."

The answer is written on the heart of each of us. As you examine your hearts, search your minds, and declare yourselves, I must say unequivocally that I cannot support a military response to the terrorist reality.

Neither my faith, my understanding of post–World War II history, nor my love of this nation's great ideals will permit me the luxury of silence. Such silence could be misconstrued as support for actions I believe to be contrary to the teachings of Jesus and antithetical to the long-term interest of human beings around the globe.

Jesus has claimed me; I am his. He taught his followers "Love your enemies and pray for those who persecute you, so that you may be children of your Father in heaven" (Matthew 5:44).

With profound sadness of heart but with hope that is anchored in the nonviolent power of resurrection, I must say *No*. Do not count me among those who in the name of religion or patriotism support this war. I cannot. This No is not a response of fear but of love and commitment to peace with justice for all people.

And then, in an attempt to educate our constituency, the following was published on November 16, 2001.

Historically, four theories or processes of informed thinking have been employed to support or oppose war.

The *crusade or holy war* theory assumes that one side is so righteous, so godly, and the other so wrong, evil even, that "they," the infidels, must be laid asunder and brought into compliance with the truth of those who adjudge themselves to be righteous.

The theory of *political necessity or national expediency* found expression initially in the writings of Machiavelli. Bluntly stated, this theory affirms "my country right or wrong" and goes for the jugular of the enemy in order to preserve or foster a way of life, to conserve or expand national boundaries, and/or to eliminate those who are in the way of jingoistic national or group interest.

The Church has not [affirmed] and does not affirm either of these two theories. They are antithetical to the gospel and the politics of the kingdom of God as revealed in Jesus.

History is tainted, however, with ugly examples of a portion of the Church's witness caving in to both holy crusades and Machiavellian thinking and practice. But such thinking and such abhorrent behavior are not representative of the Church's theology, ethics, or ethos. Rather, the Church most often is stretched in tension between the other two theories. They are the *just war theory* and various shades of *pacifism*.

Just war thinking is at the heart of Roman Catholic ethical teaching and is the accepted theory of Anglican, Presbyterian, Lutheran, and a host of the more conservative or fundamental denominations.

While there are the historic "peace churches," most notably Quakers and Mennonites, which are absolutely pacifistic, United Methodism leans toward situational pacifism but provides room for those who espouse just war thinking and behavior. (See *The Book of Discipline of The United Methodist Church, 2000,* Social Principles, paragraphs 164.G and 165.C, pages 119 and 121.)

Just war theory is not anti-peace. Rather, this understanding presupposes that there are some situations in which war is less wrong than not fighting. Wars can be justly fought, this theory affirms, if an entire set of criteria is met before war is declared and as war is conducted.

These criteria are: (1) Just cause; (2) Just intent; (3) Last resort; (4) Legitimate authority; (5) Reasonable hope of success; (6) Discrimination—meaning, immunity of noncombatants from direct attack; and (7) Proportionality—meaning the amount of damage inflicted must be strictly proportionate to the ends sought.

Opponents of the just war theory ask if any war can be just or if these criteria have a chance of being fairly assessed in the emotional context of preparing for and the fighting of a war.

Pacifism is the refusal to take life, hence, absolute pacifists will not kill under any circumstance. They understand all wars to be wrong and all killing to be sinful. Situational pacifists (and I am one) affirm that killing is always sinful, but that there may be certain extreme situations where not to take life is more evil—more sinful—than life taking (Dietrich Bonhoeffer thus participated in the plot to kill Adolf Hitler, saying the plot was sinful but to do nothing was worse).

Pacifists stake their positions on the teachings of Jesus—especially the Sermon on the Mount and on Jesus' own example of nonviolence. Pacifism also reflects the tradition of the early church. The early church practiced total pacifism until very late in the fourth century.

My expressed opposition to the present military operation in Afghanistan is not a condoning of terrorism. Quite to the contrary. I condemn terrorism in all forms. Terrorists must be brought to justice. Rather, I oppose the present military operation, as a Christian and a bishop of the Church, from the vantage point of just war criteria and my commitment to situational pacifism.

As a situational pacifist, I cannot justify the killing of civilians—especially poor and oppressed Afghan children and women. They are far more than mere "collateral damage." The end does not justify the means when human beings are involved.

The just war criteria of discrimination and proportionality are not being met in this present war. To kill innocent civilians, while tracking Osama bin Laden, and to lay waste to an oppressed, desolate country in the process runs counter to at least two of the just war criteria.

The use of United States firepower is only creating additional monstrous circumstances from which additional, long-term monstrous deeds will emerge just as the Gulf War, the embargo of Iraq, and the failure to broker a just peace between Israel and Palestine have helped to make terrorism against this nation justifiable in the minds of many fundamentalist Muslims.

Many ask, "But, even if war is wrong, what should we do now that terror has struck?"

My responses are these. Bring Osama bin Laden and his network to justice through international processes. Broker a just peace in the Middle East. Quit "bedding down" with oppressive regimes in the Islamic world. Lift the embargos on Cuba and Iraq; eliminate this form of legalized terror. And bomb Afghanistan! Bomb Afghanistan with food. Bomb Afghanistan with medicine. Bomb Afghanistan with agricultural know-how. Bomb Afghanistan with resources for public education. Bomb Afghanistan with the diplomatic and political wherewithal for women and minority groups to find their rightful place at the table of a future Afghanistan. Bomb Afghanistan with tangible expressions of love and mercy, and justice will have a chance to be done!

What we have before us . . . is an intelligence and diplomatic tragedy. But it could be turned into a victory for the whole world if the best of the teachings of Mohammed, the incarnational example of Jesus, and the power of God to reveal truth were acknowledged and followed by those who shout either Allah the Great or God Bless America.

I believe such a miracle journey is possible. It must begin with you and me. Now is the time for the whole Church to reveal the Jesus Way of peace with justice. It is time to walk the talk.

Given these writings and several sermons and speeches opposing this war, some critics charged that I failed to adhere to the just war theory they assume is at the heart of United Methodism. I dissent from their application of the just war theory in the present war and from their understanding of the United Methodist position on war and peace. To read *The Book of Discipline of The United Methodist Church, 2000* is to realize that we are not necessarily a just war Church. This war fails to adhere to the criteria of the just war theory. A letter to several publications, written in Lent, 2002, addresses these matters and more.

I write to challenge three assumptions that are abroad in today's Church in the United States and that are finding voice in Church publications. The assumption are these: (1) that the present war in Afghanistan finds validation in the just war theory; (2) that the November Pastoral Letter of the Council of Bishops of The United Methodist Church lacks theological insight; and (3) that the tepid theological and political middle ground is where the vast majority of Christians are and should be regarding the war and other related issues.

First, given the body count of noncombatants in Afghanistan, a count gleaned from U.S. media sources, that at least equals the number of persons killed in this nation by terrorists in 9/11, and given the presence of 14,000 U.S. cluster bombs nestled in 118 locations in Afghanistan with their bright hues that attract children to their maiming and killing power, and given the further devastation of a bleak landscape in the unsuccessful hunt for Osama bin Laden and his henchmen, the just war criteria of proportionality and discrimination have not been and are not being met in this war. The Church historically has said that a war is just *only* when all seven criteria of the just war theory are met before and during the fighting of a war. Clearly, this is not the case in Afghanistan. Further, the just war theory is to be employed only *after* all nonmilitary means for seeking peace with justice have been exhausted. The rush to war in Afghanistan hardly allowed for nonmilitary means to be employed before the killing began. That this nation intends to fight and expand this war is undeniable. But that such behavior should be blessed by the Church under the rubric of a just war flies in the face of the correct application of this historic theory.

Second, it was I who knowingly initiated the action that altered the original language of the Pastoral Letter of the United Methodist Council of Bishops. My motion changed our condemnation of terrorism in particular to a refutation of violence in general. The statement condemns violence in all its virulent forms, including acts of terrorism. Surely any thinking, feeling, and loving person, let alone Christians who have been taught that every war is a civil war and that each human being is a gift of God, knows that acts of terrorism are heinous wrongs to be opposed unequivocally. However, to fail to connect horrific acts of terrorism with a culture of violence and a climate that fosters death-dealing machinations is myopic at best.

Monstrous situations beget monstrous deeds. There is a direct connection between the horror of 9/11 and the failure of this nation to broker a just peace in Palestine, between the senseless killings in New York and Washington and the estimated deaths of 5,000 Iraqi civilians each month since the Gulf War ended because of the U.S. imposed embargo, and between the hatred of much of the Islamic world for the West and the presence of the Western four Ms—MTV, Militarism, McDonalds, and Michelob—wherever angry and frustrated Muslims look. Surely perceptive Christians see the link between calloused killings by terrorists and state-sanctioned violence around the globe, including this nation's embrace of capital punishment, its rush to incarcerate young men of color, and a proposed national budget that elevates military might to the status of a god. When the U.S. military budget for the next fiscal year is projected at 40 billion dollars in excess of the total military expenditures of the next nine nations combined, this nation has been seduced by a modern idolatry. Why do we wonder that many Muslims hate our "Christian" values?

The Bible and tradition teach that the church is to be a harbinger of a radically different way, a new order that was glimpsed in Jesus and is anticipated on earth as it is in heaven. This is the Church's compelling vision, that for which we yearn and that which we are to teach, preach, and embody. It is not laudable that most of the Church in the U.S. has become mute as regards our compelling vision, the radical ethos of Jesus, since 9/11.

I fail to see how an uncritical embrace of the present war hysteria resonates with the teachings and example of Jesus, honors either the pacifism of the first four centuries of the early church or the rightful application of the just war theory, acknowledges the applause we give to nonviolence each January 17, is informed by the peace statements of many of our denominations and, perhaps most tellingly, correlates with the biblical trajectory of God's *hesed* and *agape* that found perfect expression in Jesus, whom we claim as Savior and Model.

Third, it is no small thing to walk on eggs and crack none. This is adroit institutional maneuvering, if not a self-serving and rather smug way to claim the middle as sacred while assigning to the edges some kind of egg-breaking malevolence. "If only the bishops would recognize and reflect the broad middle, that solid core of collective wisdom," is the oft stated argument.

I dissent from such poppycock. There were innumerable safe voices that counseled the quiet squishy middle as lives were being eradicated in Vietnam. Martin Luther King, Jr.'s *Letter* from that infamous jail spoke truth to the falsity of the quiet middle where many whites huddled, while black people were being sacrificed on the altar of bigotry. Liberationists and feminists wonder where the silent middle is as Latin America is raped by elitism, and women struggle for the recognition God has given already. The silent middle is hardly benign territory. What affects one directly affects all indirectly, whether we like it or not.

God's arm always bends toward love, mercy, and justice. In the long run God is the ruler yet. The biblical God always asks, "Where were my people when they were needed most?" Too often, we are found sitting smugly and quietly in the safe middle—picking blackberries, as the poet once noted.

United Methodists, who sit in the middle today, either actively supporting the war or quietly acquiescing in the face of blatant war hysteria, would do well to struggle with our Church's Social Principles.

Supporters of the war, including Good News-ers, are correct to a degree. *The Discipline* does say, "Some of us believe that war, and other acts of violence, are never acceptable to Christians. We also acknowledge that most Christians regretfully realize that, when peaceful alternatives have failed, the force of arms may be preferable to unchecked aggression" (Paragraph 164.G, page 119, *The Book of Discipline of The United Methodist Church, 2000*).

But the *Discipline* does not stop there. It continues, "We believe war is incompatible with the teachings and example of Christ. We therefore reject was as a usual instrument of national foreign policy and insist that the first moral duty of all nations is to resolve by peaceful means every dispute that arises" (Paragraph 165.C, page 121).

The Pastoral Letter of the Council of Bishops reflects current United Methodist Church teaching accurately, if not courageously. From my perspective it simply does not go far enough in claiming that teaching and condemning an unwise and unjust war. I say to those who would hide in the silent center, while the war continues and a debate about it is treated as unpatriotic, that history reminds us that the silence of good people provides space for evil to take root and grow.

Finally, when renewing our baptismal vows, we United Methodists are admonished to "Remember your baptism, and be thankful."

I fear that far too often we forget our baptism in Christ but remember and are claimed by the cultural and national biases that abound. Idolatry is alive and well in us and around us.

I have maintained since 9/11 that the plight of Palestinians and the U.S. support of Israeli wrongdoing have exacerbated the hatred of our nation by some Muslims. Both 9/11 and the Middle East are part of one swatch of cloth. Thus, in the midst of the war in Afghanistan, as Israel and the Palestinians went to war, I wrote the following on April 12, 2002.

Sensitive Christians continue to live in the shadow of the Holocaust. The whole Church, save for a precious few, was complicit in this unspeakable horror. This complicity was evident in a malignant period of silence and through an ill-informed theology that affirmed two kingdoms and identified Jews as "Christ-killers," while advocating that the Jewish people stood outside God's plan for salvation. And the Western world, supposedly Christian in the early decades of the twentieth century, turned its collective back on the plight of Jews as the slaughter was planned and perpetrated. "Never Again." To be sure. No Christian could disagree.

Additionally, following Vatican II, not only did Catholics and Protestants come to view each other differently and much better, but, as Christians together, we saw and treated the Jewish community as part of, indeed as the original partner in, God's plan for salvation. This understanding took deeper root as Christians and Jews stood side by side on various justice issues, most notably civil rights and the nonviolent attack on racial segregation in this nation.

All of this and more have made it difficult for the progressive voice of the Christian community to speak out regarding the present war in the Middle East. We fear our own demons: never again do we want to be seduced by anti-Jewish attitudes and subsequent actions. Yet, it is clear that something is amiss in the Middle East. None of us condones terrorism with its suicide bombers, who maim and kill in wanton fashion. But, we have heard and seen firsthand and secondhand the plight of Palestinians, both Christians and Muslims. Present actions of some Palestinians are acts of political desperation that in part are promulgated by a balance of power tipped heavily in Israel's favor largely because of United States military hardware and this nation's financial and media backing of Israel. Another way must be found and embraced. Moderate Israelis and Palestinians have known for years what that way is. Namely:

(1) The recognition by the Palestinians and the whole Arab world of Israel's right to exist, complete with a "nonviolent" pact intact to protect all Israelis;

(2) The recognition of a Palestinian state within the pre-1967 boundaries complete with the abandonment and dismantling of the Jewish settlements in rightful Palestinian territory; and,

(3) A negotiated, United Nations–protected sharing of the Holy City.

To cry "Terrorism," as our government does, without holding Israel accountable for its state-sanctioned violence is a one-sided United States policy that only worsens the situation. Terrorism comes in many forms, including both suicide bombers and state sanctioned military violence. Both sides and this nation, which must play a major role with the Arab world in brokering a just peace, bear responsibility for the present carnage. There are no clean hands here.

It is not anti-Semitic for the Church to pray and say, "Stop the carnage and negotiate, now, in the name of God. Suicide bombs and rolling tanks are both wrong."

The struggle between the West and Islam will not be won by war(s). A hopeful future lies in creative, informed diplomacy that brokers a just peace in the Middle East and brings terrorists to justice through United Nations–sanctioned international processes while enabling serious conversations of mutual self-interest with the Islamic world.

I have returned from Afghanistan where I was part of a nineteen-person interfaith delegation recruited by Global Exchange, an energetic, young organization committed to sowing seeds of understanding and possible peace between diverse peoples and their nations.

Our delegation was Christian, Jewish, and Islamic. We were lay and clergy, Roman Catholic and Protestant. Included among us were two women who had lost siblings on 9/11 and an Afghan woman with dual citizenship in the United States and Afghanistan.

Few of us had met previously. I knew none of my colleagues before we met en route to Kabul. But, we became a community of believers, believers in the one God of all, believers in each other, and believers in the Afghan people whose suffering is incomprehensible and whose story is seldom told and hardly known in the churches of this nation. Seldom do we in the West know details of Islamic nations that are distant in geography and not part of the world's power elite.

Most assuredly, a brief visit does not make one an expert on the nation visited. I am not an Afghan expert, but I do profess a deepened understanding of that fragile nation, its people, and the present war on terrorism. As a result, I confess that my faith, coupled with heightened insight, demands not only that I seek to tell the Afghan story but also that I dare unashamedly to proffer an agenda of response for the churches and government of this nation.

A detailed history of Afghanistan can be garnered from innumerable books and accessed through Global Exchange's website at www.globalexchange.org. What follows is but a brief synopsis of that ravaged nation's history, the understanding of which is a necessity if viable options are to be envisioned, let alone embraced.

Emerging from British dominance and playing a buffer role between the national interests of Britain and Russia, Afghanistan's monarchy was established in 1919. Until 1978, a proud and productive culture emerged. Agriculture flourished, art and poetry flowered, and Kabul was an appealing city complete with a majestic palace (in the ruins of which we walked in amazement) with surrounding gardens, roads, and a mountainous vista like few in the world.

All of this changed in a dramatic eye's twinkling. Misery replaced majesty as communism subsumed the former ways and the Soviet Union invaded Afghanistan in 1979. What would be a ten-year war ensued. This devastating war (a memorial to which is the empty battle-weary, fortress-like Soviet compound on the outskirts of Kabul) was fought between the military might of the Soviet Union and the freedom fighters of Afghanistan (and the surrounding region), called the Mujahideen. Afghanistan was the Soviet Union's Vietnam. With defeat there in 1989 and escalating problems at home, the Soviet Union subsequently collapsed.

The United States played a major role in the defeat of the Soviet Union in Afghanistan. Money and training, military intelligence and strategy were provided by the United States to the Mujahideen, including a rich, Saudi, Islamic fundamentalist by the name of Osama bin Ladin. Such aid flowed through our regional allies, particularly Pakistan and Saudi Arabia.

Once the Soviets left in shame and defeat, U.S. interest waned and with it so did an outside stabilizing presence. U.S. withdrawal took with it the monetary aid so necessary for an agenda of national reformation and rebuilding. U.S. absence in Afghanistan paved the way for an extended period of devastating factional fighting that first paralyzed and then obliterated the nation's infrastructure.

The Northern Alliance, a gang of thuggish warlords, and the Mujahideen, by now an emerging coalition of young Islamic fundamentalists from the refugee camps and radical schools in Pakistan and elsewhere, fought one another viciously, while plundering the land and its people. As a result, a once proud nation literally was reduced to rubble, while the world yawned, if it even noticed. Thus, factional fighting, the scars of which pock-mark all of Afghanistan today, destroyed the nation's lifelines of art, poetry, health, education, transportation, agriculture, and trade.

The human toll exacted by those years of war is staggering, even incomprehensible, for the Western mind to conceive. That is, of a population of 22.5 million people, nearly two million were killed, another two million injured, six million driven from their homes as refugees, and an additional two million became displaced persons. In short, one-half of Afghanistan's people were directly affected by the terrors of war. Additionally, half of the nation's twenty-four thousand villages were destroyed, immense portions of the cities reduced to rubble, roads obliterated (save a very rough piece of asphalt, stone, and potholes that runs out of Kabul), and countless farms rendered untillable because of the more than two million land mines and other destructive ordnances planted and strewn across a once majestic land.

All of this has produced horrifying statistics that assault the mind and break the heart: (1) the world's largest refugee population, (2) only 36 percent adult literacy, (3) a mere $180 per capita income, (4) safe drinking water for only 13 percent of the population, (5) safe sanitation coverage for only 12 percent of the population, (6) "wasting" suffered by 25 percent of children, (7) the world's fourth worst infant mortality rate, (8) childbirth death rate of sixteen thousand mothers per year, (9) malnourishment in 70 percent of the population, and (10) an average life-expectancy of forty-five years.

It was such chaos that made possible the development of the hated and vicious Taliban, a group of fundamentalist Islamic students, 20 to 30 years of age, ignorant but passionate, who emerged from internal disputes within the Mujahideen. The bastardized brand of Islam perpetrated on the nation by these radical extremists is hardly recognizable to the scholars and essential tenets of Islam. Their brand of Islam, coupled with a vicious dictatorial style, kept the Northern Alliance at bay, crushed public dissent, and brought repression and utter despair to the people. Women in particular suffered every imaginable degradation at the hands of these much hated, but more feared, young terrorists.

Interestingly, given these staggering realities, recent developments, and U.S. governmental rhetoric, the Bush Administration provided the Taliban with $43 million as late as July 2001, in part because the Taliban did crack down on opium production (75 percent of all poppy seeds needed for opium production were grown in Afghanistan).

The Afghan people, on September 11, 2001, had experienced three consecutive years of drought (a plague that continues today) in a nation in which 85 percent of the population is agriculture-dependent. This formidable reality was set in the midst of twenty-three consecutive years of war. And, then, in October 2001, the hunt for Osama bin Laden brought the United States war planes that, while rightly driving out the hated Taliban to the people's general delight, nevertheless, continued the death-dealing destruction that the land and people of Afghanistan had endured for longer than either ecological balance or human ingenuity could hope to survive.

The "War on Terrorism" was unleashed on the people of Afghanistan because the Taliban would not surrender Osama bin Laden and his henchmen. The bombing began and continued in an aggressive, invasive attempt to kill him and his cadre of confidants, while also intending to destroy the entire al-Qaida network of terror.

Undoubtedly bin Laden and al-Qaida were at the heart of the 9/11 tragedy, thus making their demise a laudable goal. They should be brought to justice through an international police process that is in effect for bringing to justice such vicious rogues. They rightly need to be eliminated as a force of evil in the world. But, what the U.S. government either did not understand or failed to acknowledge in its bellicose response was that the Taliban could not or would not surrender bin Laden. He was too important to them.

The concentric circles of power and influence in Afghanistan in the fall of 2001 were these: (1) Osama bin Laden and his Saudi and Yemen elite at the center; (2) al-Qaida, the network of young Islamic extremists trained in the radical schools in Pakistan. These warriors emanate from bin Laden, while few of them have seen him or his core elite; (3) the Taliban, whom bin Laden financed, influenced, manipulated, and into whose core he married; and finally, (4) the people of Afghanistan who became, once again, pawns in the war games of other power players. Tragically, they paid, and continue to pay, for the diabolical acts of others.

Undeniably, in the hunt for bin Laden, the understandable desire to eradicate al-Qaida, and the laudable commitment to dismantle the Taliban, it was the common people of Afghanistan who bore the brunt of the U.S. military response.

Estimates of the loss of innocent lives due to human error and carelessness in U.S. bombing raids vary from one thousand to four thousand. Presently, village to village survey crews working in the devastated areas, led by a team from Global Exchange, have documented the deaths of some one thousand people as a result of U.S. military action. They estimate the toll to be nearer to four thousand, but because entire villages were obliterated in the bombing, few eye witnesses have been found in the more extreme southern areas where devastation is rampant. Few surveyors or key witnesses believe the killings were intentional. Rather, most believe they were the results of human error and military carelessness.

Our delegation heard firsthand reports of some of the verifiable losses. Our sources included:

(1) A ten-year-old boy who drew for me the Guernica-like portrayal of death that now hangs on the wall of my home study. With crayons and paper our delegation provided and while seated with me on the hard floor of a mental hospital ward used occasionally as an out-patient unit to hear the stories of victims' families, he drew in deft, left-handed images horrific visuals of what it was like for him

and his younger sister to watch the bombs fall on their father, mother, siblings, and farm animals. He does not hate the United States; he only yearns to have his parents back. His picture screams at me. It plaintively asks, Should any child ever have to draw a picture depicting the mangled, disconnected body parts of parents? Siblings? Even farm animals? I think not.

(2) A seven-year-old girl who was making tea for relatives in the kitchen adjacent to her family home in a tiny southern village when she saw the airplanes and experienced three waves of air strikes before discovering the bodies of her mother and thirteen additional family members. "I hate the U.S.," she said. "They killed my mother. Why did they kill my family?" "We are so sorry," we responded. One of us, a veteran Roman Catholic peace advocate and a stateswoman *par excellence* offered, "I have a granddaughter your age. She has cried and prayed for the children of Afghanistan since the bombing began. She would want me to tell you how sad and sorry she is." After a pause, the beautiful Afghan child said, "Tell her thanks."

(3) A ten-year-old fourth grader whose lofty test scores suggest he belongs in the seventh grade. He was so excited to be back in school that he and his cousin left early that day. On the way to school his cousin picked up a bright yellow object and tossed it to the ten-year-old. The U.S. bomblet, one of 202 contained in a cluster bomb, exploded, ripping at the young boy's body. Inadequate local health care providers suggested that both arms and legs be amputated. The parents resisted. In the midst of the debate it was discovered that Germany has a surgery program for just such victims. Thus, for three months, this precocious ten-year-old was in a hospital in Germany. Today, his scarred arms and damaged legs are intact. He can walk, even run, and return to school. He asked, given what was done to him, what we and the United States intend to do

for him and his people. He told us that most of his friends are dead and that he is afraid to go outside to play. He seldom touches the earth for fear it will explode. We responded with promises we intend to keep (including this article). Smilingly he said, "When I grow up, like you, I'll make Afghanistan into gold."

Our delegation was privileged to witness the detonation of the one millionth land mine found and then destroyed by the HALO Trust, a British Non-Governmental Organization (NGO), made popular by Princess Diana.

It was a frightful experience to be 10 feet from a live minefield and then, later, to experience HALO's detonation of the one millionth land mine worldwide. Eight hundred sixty thousand of these death-dealing devices have been located and destroyed in Afghanistan alone. The miners, who find and destroy these lethal weapons, are young men, 20 to 30 years of age, who leave their Afghan families to work at probing for land mines 22 out of 30 days each month. They receive $130 per month for this dangerous work.

They seek out devices of death planted or dropped by successive waves of Russians, Northern Alliance, Mujahideen, Taliban, and Americans. They estimate that at least 1.25 million ordnances of destruction are strewn across the rubble or planted in the farmlands of Afghanistan.

Embracing these warriors for peace, our delegation applauded them for being the heroes they are. They responded that what they do is necessary work that needs to be done for the future of their beloved country and its people.

Their leader, a middle-aged Afghan medical doctor, whose gentle spirit, profound courage, and quick mind touched all of us, when asked how his Islamic faith influenced his work, said, "There is but one trunk with many branches. We all belong to the same God. We welcome your Christian concern for Muslims and this country."

He continued, "If you really want to help, if you want to eradicate terror and defeat the Taliban, tell the American people how good you have it and ask them to help abolish poverty. After all poverty is the root cause of all suffering."

Monstrous circumstances do produce monsters and monstrous deeds.

I went to Afghanistan opposing Mr. Bush's self-declared "War on Terrorism." I still oppose his methodology. However, the visit to Afghanistan has taught me much and challenged my situational pacifism in a quite specific manner.

Person after person, while not affirming the U.S. bombing, applauded the demise of the Taliban and urged us to push our government not to leave Afghanistan but, instead, to join with other nations in the global community to provide a long-term security force that would preserve peace and guarantee adequate time for the new government to evolve so that Afghanistan might be rebuilt by the Afghan people with help from the global community.

As a result, I offer the following strategies for peace in Afghanistan and the eradication of terror in the region.

(1) Given the history and present situation, the world community, including the U.S., must commit to the presence of a long-term peace-keeping force through the maintenance of the International Security Assistance Force. The historic Loya Jirga's quite recent work of selecting a new government led by President Hamid Karzai must be given a chance to succeed. The presence of the warlords of the Northern Alliance in the government, the potential money to be made from chaos and drugs, and the threat of the Taliban's possible return all argue for the presence of a security force that cannot be bought and that will maintain order. Sometimes persuasive force is necessary.

(2) Given the indescribable devastation across the nation, a new Marshall Plan is needed for Afghanistan. These are proud, hard-working, and brilliant people. They want to rebuild their country. They can do it if the tools of technology, grain, health care, food, medicine, education, and time are provided. Once again, it is in our hands to do. The question of the small child is right, "Since you bombed us, will you build us and give us a chance?"

(3) Refugee camps must be emptied in Afghanistan, the region, and Palestine. They are cesspools that breed extremism as every imaginable human deprivation is perpetrated and experienced, thus engaging the young and establishing a context where terrorism is conceived and nurtured. People must be helped to return home to land and hope. Our surest defense against terrorism will never be found in bombs and bullets but in long-term, sustained involvement in the lives of people for whom hope long ago took flight on the wings of failed promises.

(4) The U.S. government should immediately (and the churches demand that it does) establish and deploy a $25 million Victim's Compensation Fund. Let's acknowledge our mistakes and make amends to the families of victims. The gesture will speak a thousand truths, while providing much needed capital for the rebuilding underway.

(5) Church groups need to go to Afghanistan, now. Go to sow seeds of understanding and peace. The American people, especially those from faith-based communities, care. We can communicate love and commitment because these verities abide at the heart of all that is right in our faith commitments. The people of Afghanistan will respond positively. We do not need to go to proselytize Muslims. God's work of salvation will be done by God through Islamic hands. But the incarnation of the gospel is much needed. The people of Afghanistan need to experience servant lead-

ership, actualized *agape* and *hesed* in faith-based communities committed to the least, last, and lost. Such gifts are at the heart of the gospel. The church has invaluable gifts to give.

(6) NGOs must go to and stay in Afghanistan long term. Groups like Catholic Relief, Church World Service, and Volunteers in Mission should commit to Afghanistan for the long haul and join the many NGOs presently there. NGO expertise is welcomed and needed.

(7) People of goodwill must hold the U.S. government's feet to the fire of tangible commitment. We must not abandon these people again lest all hell break loose in the region and this fragile nation disappear from the face of the earth.

The concluding event for our delegation was an interfaith service of prayer and healing with Afghan family members who have lost loved ones in the wars, generally, and in the bombing campaign, specifically.

It was an incredible experience as the blind Mullah chanted and sang Islamic death liturgies; as the two women of our delegation who had lost siblings on 9/11 spoke eloquently and sang passionately; as Jews, Christians, and Muslims prayed together and embraced unashamedly.

It was my profound privilege to speak the concluding words for our delegation. There in the rubble, in the midst of unspeakable horror and unimaginable anguish, these were my words:

"There is a place in my heart where two rivers run together. Each river is different from the other: One is deep, green, and quiet; the other shallow, blue, and rushing. Where they come together is a place of mystery, chaos, and miracle. It is a sacred place, a place of God.

"We gather as two different streams of God's one river of humanity. Each of us is different in culture, dress,

language, religion, and life experience. We cannot compre-
hend the depth of your suffering across these twenty-three
years of war. Our way of life in the United States is difficult
for you to understand. We are very different streams of life.
Yet, here today, in this place, we come together in shared
grief, common prayer, and unified hope for our nations
and their people.

"Together, we believe that this place of confluence is a
place of miracle and mystery where God intends to do a
new thing, turning suffering to hope and tears to laughter.

"May it be so for your sake, our sake, the humility of the
U.S., the peace with justice of Afghanistan, and the joy of
your precious, beautiful, and magnificent children.
SALAAM."

As the blind Mullah embraced, kissed, and thanked me,
and I him, with my young artist friend hand-in-hand, I
believed then, and I continue to believe now, that a new day
in Afghanistan is possible if the world cares and people of
faith do not permit the U.S. government to forget and for-
sake the fragile and broken little ones of God's good creation. Not to forget but to act will be the first step for all of
us to sow seeds of understanding and peace. May it be so for
God's sake, the people of Afghanistan, and our very souls.

It was in that restaurant in 1951 that the demon of racism
stole my innocence. That same demon determined the creation of the Methodist Central Jurisdiction in 1939. It lurks,
today, in the shadows of racial profiling and raises its ugly
head as nonsuburban public school systems bear the brunt
of ethnic and racial marginalization of most young people of
color in this nation. I have never been able to understand
how Christians could remain complacent in the face of racial
prejudices and racist practices. Consider these words from a
1998 report from the Milton S. Eisenhower Foundation as
quoted by Erna Paris in her recent book, *Long Shadows:*

The foundation recorded that in spite of the emergence of a larger African American middle class and improving high school graduation rates, unemployment in the inner cities of America was at Depression-era levels. . . . The child-poverty level in the United States was four times higher than in Western Europe, and the rate of incarceration of African American men (is) four times higher than it was in apartheid South Africa. A black child born in Washington or Harlem had a lower life expectancy than a child born in Bangladesh.[1]

Martin Luther King, Jr.'s words that confronted the latent prejudices and assaulted the acquiescence to systemic racism at the beginning of my ministry still ring true today. He said that we Christians, and the whole church, are too often anvils of the status quo instead of hammers for justice, thermometers for what "is" instead of thermostats for what God intends.

Racism remains the terminal social cancer that eats at the soul of this nation. If Christians do not put everything at our disposal on the line for the actualization of kingdom/reign of God politics in which color evaporates as the primary indicator of opportunity, this nation will continue its plunge into that catastrophic abyss where fearful Anglos continue to run in order to escape "them," while leaving behind center cities and first rung suburbs that are pockets of decay. These have become the tough neighborhoods where people of color are expected to become model citizens while renewing these neighborhoods despite a woeful lack of much needed financial and leadership resources.

The church must model a new paradigm of possibility and this requires more than occasional bursts of pious rhetoric, periodic judicatory resolutions, a few media-oriented events or the elevation of a desired quota of leaders

---

1. Erna Paris, *Long Shadows: Truth, Lies and History* (New York: Bloomsbury, 2000), pp. 174-75.

of color to places of prominence and power. It means, instead, reorienting ourselves as to what evangelism and mission are. It means the deployment of significant financial and human resources, as part and parcel of who we are as church, for the recruitment, training, and nurture of a new generation of leaders of color. And it means that we take the risk of reinvesting some of our considerable financial assets in those often forsaken neighborhoods, while pushing the governments of cities, counties, and this nation to do the same.

Race matters in the church and this culture. We cannot pretend to be followers of Jesus if our prejudices are not exorcized and the demon of racism sent back to the Sea from whence it came. Pure and simple, racism is evil incarnate. The elimination of our color-driven biases and systemic patterns of white privilege and the oppression of people of color must be at the top of the United Methodist agenda, as well as that of the whole church and this nation.

This means being attentive to our criminal justice system. Instead of building more prisons for young men of color, while providing demeaning jobs for poor whites to maintain them, we must declare a sustained and winnable war on racism and poverty. We must address the gap that is rapidly becoming a chasm between the haves and have-nots through a resolute commitment to eliminate the root causes of poverty and racism. This cannot be accomplished successfully through underfunded faith-based initiatives. What is needed is a major private-public assault on the evils of unemployment; inadequate education; hunger; substandard housing; inaccessible health care; drugs; HIV/AIDS; absent fathers; abandoned youth; and brutal violence whether from gangs, police departments, or the renewed frenzy for capital punishment.

The events of 9/11 have shown us the utter absurdity of violence. Given its sinful virulence, whether legally sanctioned by the state or clandestinely practiced by terrorists, I am a situational pacifist. That is, while there are paradoxical situations where life-taking may be the least hurtful choice among available options, nevertheless I find most acts of violence, as well as this nation's dependency on military might, incompatible with Christian teaching. I cannot understand how Christians have been seduced so easily by the false god of militarism; 9/11 has rendered the nonviolent, prophetic voice of the church nearly mute. How quickly we forget.

The ministry of Jesus, the pacifism of the early church, and the recent voice of Martin Luther King, Jr. expose our complicity with such systemic violence. As a Christian who protests our national love affair with violence, and as one who advocates Jesus' course of nonviolence, I wonder what the news stories would be in the Islamic world, Latin America, Africa (especially Angola), Vietnam, Cambodia, not to mention the streets and public housing units of our urban areas, if this nation were to invest a fraction of the military budget in programs that address unmet human needs. The War on Poverty remains the only underfunded war in our nation's history. One wonders what our history would have been if we had disengaged militarily from the Middle East, Vietnam, and the Gulf War, as quickly as we disengaged from the War on Poverty or with the determination with which we seem to be intent on engaging in conflict with a sizable portion of the Islamic world. War, race, and violence are inseparably part of the seamless garment of issues that cannot be separated from each other lest the whole fabric unravel.

As the violence of capital punishment is part and parcel of this seamless composite, given the disproportionate number of poor black and brown men on the death rows of this nation, so too is the practice of abortion. I believe that, like our stated positions on war and peace, race, capital punishment, and poverty, the United Methodist position on abortion (Paragraph 161.J, page 102, *The Book of*

Discipline of The United Methodist Church, 2000) is on target. It is a pastoral position that, like our position opposing capital punishment, recognizes the sacred character of life and opposes abortion as an easy out for irresponsible behavior. This statement is neither rigidly pro-life nor rigidly pro-choice. Our position faces the hard fact that, in some situations, life does so conflict with life, physically and/or qualitatively, that a decision to abort, while never easy and always emotionally and spiritually hurtful, may be the most loving and viable option available. Such a realistic pastoral position, anchored in the gospel of love and augmented by the inescapable need for humans to make difficult choices, is a gift to the abortion debate. The shame is that too few United Methodists know our position or have the courage to offer it, if they do. While I cannot treat abortion as an issue of mere individual choice or a means of birth control, and, while I do oppose a casual affirmation of abortion as a personal right independent of other considerations, I do understand and support abortion as the most loving option in some quite limited situations.

These several issues, as well as others such as general amnesty for immigrants, debt relief for Third World nations, the rights of women and children, claim my attention and are part of that seamless garment which is the tapestry for God's inclusive, hospitable table of the kingdom/reign God initiated in Jesus. Given all of this, the homosexual controversy has not been for me the troubling issue it has been for many Christians. From a biblical and theological point of view I understand gay and lesbian persons to be those victims, like yesterday's lepers and today's people of color, who have been adjudged to be outsiders by the rigid, exclusive mandates of church attitudes and/or laws. I do not agree with this stance and find neoliteralist biblical understanding of the seven infamous biblical passages misguided.

The seven passages are: Genesis 19:4-11; Leviticus 18:22 and 20:13-14; Deuteronomy 23:17-18; 1 Kings 14:22-24 and 22:46; Romans 1:26-32; 1 Corinthians 6:9; and 1 Timothy 1:10. (Note that I combined the two passages in both Leviticus and 1 Kings because they address the same issue.)

The United Methodist Church, at its 1992 General Conference, received a report from the Committee to Study Homosexuality, recommending that resource materials for churches and individuals be developed. What emerged was entitled "The Church Studies Homosexuality" (Abingdon Press, 1994). Its editor and advisory committee considered carefully the experiences of hundreds of faithful church persons, and the writings of theologians and biblical scholars from the conservative end of the spectrum to the liberal, and presented both a traditional and an alternate interpretation of each of these passages. My interpretations have been drawn in part from these alternate interpretations, and from other thoughtful responses of respected teachers, among them Victor Paul Furnish and Virginia Ramey Mollenkott, whose words bear repeating:

> Many English translations of the Bible contain the word *homosexual* in extremely negative contexts. But the fact is that the word *homosexual* does not occur anywhere in the Bible. No extant text, no manuscript, neither Hebrew nor Greek, Syriac, nor Aramaic, contains the word. The terms *homosexual* and *heterosexual* were not developed in any language until the 1890s, when for the first time the awareness developed that there are people with a lifelong, constitutional orientation toward their own sex. Therefore the use of the term *homosexuality* by certain English Bible translators is an example of the extreme bias that endangers the human and civil rights (I would add church rights and privileges) of homosexual persons.[2]

---

2. Virginia Ramey Mollenkott, "Human Rights and the Golden Rule," from *Christianity and Crisis*, November 9, 1987.

Given the implication that a much more derogatory tone has been read into the ancient biblical texts by translators than was originally intended, consider the following brief interpretations that I offer on the seven passages:

Read Genesis 19:4-11 carefully. Can you imagine offering your daughters or those of anyone else for gang rape to assuage the lustfulness of an enraged mob? This is not a story about sexual orientation or the sin of gay men. Rather, this is a story about the ends to which Lot would go to protect his guests and practice the etiquette of hospitality. The mob wanted the visitors, to "know" them, not because either the guests or the mob were gay (actually the guests were angels) but in order to perform an extreme act of dehumanization on strangers. To read this story as a condemnation of gay men or a refutation of loving, committed, monogamous gay or lesbian relationships is a violation of the text itself.

The passages from Leviticus are part of the holiness code for the maintenance of spiritual purity in ancient Israel. Read these codes carefully, especially if you are a Christian. The Church has not considered these ancient laws binding on Christians in that they were laws for an emerging people in a certain time and place. Needless to say, some of these outdated laws are broken daily by most devout Christians, both progressives and neoliteralists.

The Deuteronomy and 1 Kings passages are focused on the use of male and female Israelites for prostitution, especially in the fertility practices of Israel's neighbors. Such fertility rites were understood to be idolatrous pagan practices. I agree. But I cannot imagine how such texts can be misinterpreted to suggest they speak to the issue of same sex orientation in today's world.

Romans 1:26-32 at first reading is the most serious challenge to a progressive point of view. Verses 26 and 27 in the New Revised Standard Version say: "Their women exchanged natural intercourse for unnatural, and in the same way also the men, giving up natural intercourse with women, were consumed with passion for one another. Men committed shameless acts with men and received in their own persons the due penalty for their error."

Before we interpret this passage as a blanket condemnation of homosexuality, as some do, we should note at least two telling factors. First, both women and men are condemned for giving up *natural* relations with the opposite sex. Other-gender affection is a gift, an orientation, that a gay man or lesbian woman does not have. *Natural*, for the inherently homosexual person, is same-sex affection. Second, this passage says nothing about love, especially love shared by homosexual couples but, instead, rightly focuses on lust and dishonorable passion. The emphasis is on sexual activity that is lustful and idolatrous. This text does not in any way address the issue of committed love, and subsequent sexual activity, shared by faithful gay and lesbian couples.

While Paul's denunciation of ungodliness and wickedness must be taken seriously, as part of Scripture's authority, it should not be misread to assume that Paul knew about or was speaking against same-sex orientation, love, and commitment.

First Corinthians 6:9 and 1 Timothy 1:10 contain the word "homosexual" in the Revised Standard Version, New English Bible, and Living Bible translations and "sodomite" in the New Revised Standard Version in long lists of those persons who will not inherit the kingdom of God and are named as transgressors of God's good law.

The testimony of biblical scholar Mollenkott again is helpful.

Two words in 1 Corinthians 6:9 and one word in 1 Timothy 1:10 have recently been taken to mean that homosexual people will be excluded from God's kingdom and therefore do not merit protection in the world of human experience. But well into the twentieth century the first of these Greek words, *malakos*, was unanimously understood by leaders in all religious traditions to mean *not* homosexual acts, but masturbation. There is no textual reason why the understanding of this word should recently have changed. The fact is that very few of our contemporaries, church people included, can believe that masturbation would merit exclusion from heaven. So the reading of *malakos* has been transferred to a minority group so marginalized that only a few Bible scholars and theologians have expressed outrage at such carelessness.

The second Greek word, *arsenokoites*, was taken during the first four Christian centuries to mean "male prostitute." Then as now, male prostitutes were available for hire by women as well as men. That this word should now be translated *homosexual*, as if the biblical author were talking about a permanent sexual orientation instead of a specific sex abuse, is typical of the misuse of biblical passages.[3]

These *arsenokoites*, male prostitutes, were quite likely boys. Paul very well may have been speaking against both pederasty and child prostitution. If he had intended a blanket statement aimed at all homosexuals, there are other Greek words that would have communicated this point far more clearly.

I conclude that these seven passages hardly permit or encourage the present attitudes and behavior of the Church in relation to those whose sexual orientation is same sex.

Present Church behavior toward gay and lesbian persons is akin to the earlier treatment of lepers and people of color in recent times. Do not be mistaken. I do not equate the treatment of gay and lesbian persons by the Church to compare in historic magnitude with the virulence heaped on people of color. Racism was and remains the primary

---

3. Ibid.

sin of the church and culture in the United States. But the Church's treatment of gays and lesbians is similar to our sinful practice of racism. It is based on a misunderstanding of the Bible; it negates the clear hospitable witness of Jesus; it fails to accept the preponderance of available scientific data; it perpetuates demeaning prejudices; and, it opens the door to overt and covert violence against gays and lesbians.

A key question that the Church must address is not one of sexual orientation any more than one of race or gender. Variables of sexual orientation, color, and gender are inherent givens. The Christ has broken down all dividing walls of hostility. We have been made One in baptism; therefore, the question for the Church is not one of inherent givens, but how the Church can support people, as they were created by God, as they seek in faith to make the journey of discipleship toward wholeness.

Gay men and lesbian women for the most part were born or formed early in life as those whose inherent sexual orientation is homosexual. Reversal of orientation is not possible for them. As part of God's good creation, the question for gay and lesbian persons is not who they are as sexual beings, but what they do with their special orientation in relationship to one another in the sight of and with the support of God.

The issue for the Church is not to debate sexual orientation or to judge gays and lesbians or to seek to discover how to transform them into what they are not, but rather how the Church will so welcome and support these sisters and brothers in Christ in their differences so that they will become all they can be and, thereby, encouraged and supported to live in monogamous relationships, if the gift of celibacy is not a gift God has bestowed on them.

Quite obviously, our United Methodist bans on ordination of qualified "practicing" homosexuals and union services for same-sex couples—based on the arrogant statement that we "find the practice of homosexuality incompatible with Christian teaching" (Paragraph 161.G, page 101, *The Book of Discipline of The United Methodist Church, 2000*)—are not in sync with our denomination's historic stance as a welcoming community for those most needful of nurture, support, and Christlike acceptance. Our positions on homosexuality tear at the seamless garment of our heritage. Because of this, as we presently lament our graphic racism that prompted the emergence of other Methodist denominations for black people and permitted the Central Jurisdiction to be established in 1939 (and kept in place until the merger of 1968), I believe that in the case of gay and lesbian Christians future generations of United Methodists will mourn our woeful ignorance, be deeply embarrassed by our cowardice, and engage in public acts of repentance on behalf of a minority group of people the Church once adjudged to be unclean and/or second-class.

My two arrests in Cleveland, Ohio, at the 2000 General Conference were the result of actions of pastoral solidarity with and for gay and lesbian Christians. As I had done all of my life, I stood with the outsider. Some members of the Church were outraged. Some were embarrassed. Some were proud of my behavior. I did what I did because I could not fathom a bishop doing less. Until all are welcomed, no one is at home in the Church. That is just the way it is in the kingdom/reign of God of which the Church, as the Body of Christ, is called to be the radical and courageous harbinger of God's way.

Gay and lesbian persons are part of a great line of historical splendor of those adjudged by church and culture to be outsiders and of little value, but who, in reality, are of inestimable worth to God whether we welcome them or not. God in Christ has said yes already. The only question is this: When will we finally hear the voice of the Christ and respond, "Welcome home, brothers and sisters in Christ"?

While I must dissent from United Methodism's near silence on the present war, our historic sinful treatment of people of color and our present attitudes, laws, and behavior regarding gay and lesbians, I affirm with gratitude our heritage of honoring and yearning to wear a seamless garment that will cover the needy and oppressed. Our heritage understands that to picket and pray, hold the hand and go to jail, organize the congregation and worship are part of that seamless garment in which, by grace through faith, we United Methodists are privileged to dwell. May the present tear in the garment of the Church be mended by the confluence of God's grace with the trust and obedience of all of us who name the name of Jesus as Savior and Liberator.

Conclusion

This seamless garment emerges from the water of baptism.

Baptism makes all of us one with Christ and each other. This is fundamental Christianity. Baptism demands radical social sensitivities.

Our problem is that, quite often, we forget our baptisms, but remember our cultural biases and prejudices. This is true in matters of war and violence, race and gender, poverty and sexuality, particularly homosexuality.

I affirm baptism as immersion in Christ with all of its wondrous privileges and demanding responsibilities. As I remember my baptism and am thankful, I know that faithful discipleship demands radical obedience that dares to challenge the biases and prejudices woven into the fabric of this nation, church institutions, and our very souls. It was Dietrich Bonhoeffer who wrote in *The Cost of Discipleship*, "When Christ calls a man, he bids him come and die."

Chapter Eight

To Forgo the Luxury

The Church and culture of the United States experienced cataclysmic shifts in 1968. Urban rebellions replaced the nonviolent civil disobedience of the assassinated Dreamer. And the dream, too long delayed, sought other, more strident venues for its movement from vision to reality.

Ecumenism, which at root is not merely concerned with the intracooperation and intercooperation of religious bodies, but also with the unity of the whole created order, turned outward from Catholic-Protestant living room dialogues, and choir and pulpit exchanges to embrace new organizational expressions of interdenominational and interfaith solidarity. These organizations focused their attention on the marginalized in the United States, especially black people and the oppression they had endured.

Following two urban rebellions in Cincinnati, Ohio, where I was an inner-city pastor, there emerged in November 1968, one of the earliest interfaith ministries in the nation. This ministry remains strong today. The Metropolitan Area Religious Coalition of Cincinnati (MARCC) is committed across denominational and faith lines to "forgo the luxury of separate ways when a common path can be found" for the doing of justice on behalf of the poor and marginalized in the name of God.

Our style in the late 1960s was research-action-reflection with the power brokers of the metropolis. Our research of Cincinnati's power elite taught us that, in 1968, most of the urban decision makers occupied pews in the Catholic and Protestant churches and Jewish synagogues, especially the Reform and Conservative, on Friday nights, Saturday, and Sunday mornings. Thus, we developed a sophisticated methodology for social change, complete with empowerment through increased personal relationships with the have-nots. The religiously oriented haves of the metro area were encouraged to employ their significant influence for the sake of systemic justice. I learned by experience that social change can occur when have-nots, advocating change, are assisted by well placed haves who will help to pry open doors too long closed to justice and care.

This was a period of accelerated growth and change for me. I began my work in civil rights, the anti–Vietnam War movement, and a plethora of other social justice concerns from the vantage point of standing with the poor, who were my parishioners and neighborhood friends, only to find myself at the age of twenty-nine beginning to rub shoulders with the political, economic, and other systemic power brokers of the metro area, state, and nation. This was quite a stretch for a young preacher, whose early years included project living and a monumental struggle to get to and through college and seminary. This phase in my life stamped me indelibly as a justice-seeker, yet one who learned that change occurs through coalitions, and that networks which bring lasting change often are a fusion of strange allies, especially of the powerful and powerless. The church can play a much needed brokering role in the building of these much needed alliances.

I had been pastor of the first German Methodist congregation in the world, a proud congregation that had become a home for poor white Appalachian migrants, and was a partner institution with a next-door United Methodist community center that served the poorest of the black community. Moving from that role to the position of Executive

Director of MARCC meant that my horizon shifted and broadened almost overnight. I learned that Catholics and Protestants at the grassroots level, and in offices of ecclesiastical power, were theologically similar and cared deeply about the same issues. I learned that Jews were neither Christ killers nor hell-bound, but viable, faithful children of the Covenant, who had much to teach Christians about the daily reality of doing justice. I also learned that affluent white people, at least an influential minority, can be organized as agents of change if you learn to know them, study the hard issues with them, and stand with them and the poor in fragile coalitions of mutual self-interest, support, and power for good. In the midst of this intensive period of ministry, I came to see ecumenism at root as the gift God has given and readily desires to come to fruition for the salvation of humankind and the good of the whole created order.

Commitments to the eternal verities of love, forgiveness, reconciliation, and strong familial morality were present across the spectrum of class, race, religion, and theology. When we focused on doing justice in God's world, we discovered a marvelous gift of unity inherent among us that drove us relentlessly into the future we believed God held open for all to enter.

The shame is that the United States culture shifted. With this shift, the me-ism of the Nixon and Reagan years seduced the religious communities to embrace the institutional sin of spiritual naval gazing, and all of us, Protestant, Catholic, Jewish, and other emerging religious groups, especially the Muslims, turned inward. We not only moved away from each other and the poor, but we also grappled incessantly for power and dominance within our own faith communities. Instead of struggling for justice for the have-nots, we fought internally with those who differed from us theologically and politically. We acted as if we had the luxury of parochial denominationalism. We behaved as if an expectant God and a hurting world did not need us or care if we bludgeoned each other unmercifully. We did these things and others in the name of the God whose unity we squandered. But, God continues to call us to new allegiances that transcend our petty differences. Nevertheless, in the midst of these ugly squabbles many United Methodists ask, "Will there be a schism among us?"

We have come a long way from the heady and hearty days of 1968 when we stood with a vast assemblage of other religious folks to a new millennium in which we have trouble standing together as United Methodists, let alone standing with those who differ theologically and denominationally from us.

I am not one who believes that unity can be built on the backs of a theological sellout or the least common political or social denominator. The 1939 unification of The Methodist Church built on the backs of black Methodists was a sinful sellout to racial prejudice and institutional racism. We continue to pay the price for the unexpunged results of that action. I do not believe that progressive and neoliteralist United Methodists should hide our differences on the nature of biblical authority, the thorny subject of Christology, or the differing theological-political positions our varied beliefs naturally produce. It is essential that we be courageous, vulnerable, and truthful in our dealings with one another. This I affirm, so that a candid dialogue in search of truth might occur. I protest the probability that getting ecclesiastical power instead of seeking truth has become the name of the game for too many of us. Rather than grappling across theological and denominational lines for God's truth, we are enmeshed in power games such as name-calling, vindictive journalism, and the propagation of half-truths. I presuppose that such actions do not serve God's cause, but are employed out of fear among neoliter-

alists and allowed to stand largely unchallenged by progressives because of an evasive cynicism that seems to
assume it does not matter anyhow. Progressive silence is as
sinful as neoliteralist virulence. Our behavior does matter.
How we treat each other is as important as what we say we
believe, if the gospel is to be believed and the world given
a light by which to see.

I affirm that the United Methodist tent is large enough
for wide differences in theology and politics to dwell
together in unity with tension. We are a conciliar people,
not a creedal or confessional body. But such acceptance
presupposes humility and tolerance on all sides. Humility
that understands that God has more to teach than we
know. Tolerance that realizes that others might have something to contribute to our growth and development.
Humility that is nurtured by realizing that we not only see
through a glass darkly, but also from the finite vantage
point we occupy by virtue of life experiences, theological
training, ethnicity, sexuality, geographical location, and
exposure to racial, sexual, cultural, and global differences.
Certainly, this white, male, straight bishop from Chicago,
who lived in projects as a child, has stood in picket lines,
served in several diverse settings and whose mind and
heart could never settle for pat answers, does see life and
church differently than would a bishop with far different
life experiences. We simply must learn to be tolerant of
each other. For example, my journey as a heterosexual,
married male has nevertheless put me in proximity to gay
and lesbian Christians for thirty years, largely because of
my work in urban ministry. Certainly, I see gay and lesbian
Christians differently than do those neoliteralists whose
primary experiences with gay and lesbian Christians are
largely theoretical or limited in face-to-face encounters.

As I reflect on the 1960s and early 1970s, the positive
influence of the religious community, limited as it was,

resulted largely from our collective focus on and commitment to the needs of those outside our own institutions of religion. I dissent from the palpable reality that we have lost this dimension and instead mutter and sputter with fear, cynicism, and a plethora of faddish strategies aimed at our own institutional survival, sometimes at any cost, including the sacrifice of much of that which is dear to United Methodism regarding our historic commitments to justice, diversity, and hospitality.

I affirm that, if we were to focus more on a world torn apart by suffering children, war, HIV/AIDS, hopeless refugees, poverty, hunger, poor education, meaninglessness among the affluent young, unavailable health care, the unequal distribution of land and wealth, and ecological blindness and less on fostering our narrow points of view or trying to have our candidate elected to a position of power, God would grant a new vision of unity in the midst of our very real differences. I cannot ask a neoliteralist to forgo what is sacrosanct to him or her, but I can request that we join hearts and heads in caring for the least among us. God in Christ asks no less of all of us.

If nonschism within United Methodism means that progressives must remain quiet or that the pension fund or trust clause will not let us part, then I dissent. However, I affirm that schism need not occur. There is room for us prayerfully and vulnerably to enter a new era of unity, while not sacrificing our integrity, if with a new dose of humility and tolerance we will look outward to the world John Wesley deemed his, and to our parish, and enter it together.

MARCC became more than an institution to our family. Ironically, the morning after I was appointed MARCC's first Executive Director, our young son, Mark C. Sprague, died. From Mark to MARCC. Mysteriously, trusting that God in Christ holds our beloved son, I believe that God gave us MARCC as a vehicle for expressing the wonder

and majesty of it all, despite the frailties, foibles, and fini-
tude of humankind and the institutions we help to shape.

MARCC taught me that, despite differences that are
deep and wide, people of faith not only can stand up for
others but also in the process, learn to appreciate, respect,
and even love one another. My abiding sadness with
Rome's increased rigidity, the continued rise of Zionism
within American Jewry, the emergence of a fringe element
of fanatical Muslims, and our denominational wars within
Protestantism, especially those inside United Methodism,
results from knowing that there is a better way, a way of
justice leaning toward truth. This is the way whereby the
world can see and believe, if with tolerance and humility
we will "forgo the luxury of separate ways when a common path can be found."

If we who have seen the light, however faintly, and profess to be children of the light, cannot find this common
path, how can a world, full of people shrouded in darkness, ever hope to see? Without such a path we will deserve
the schisms we create, despite God's gift of ecumenism
present among us. I affirm the available path, and I dissent
from the arrogant schism we United Methodists increasingly predict and seem addicted to embrace.

Conclusion

There is unity present in the heart of God's good, but
fallen creation. The church is called to sight, signal, and live
that new creation. When we fail to do so, we betray God.
When we behave as if strife and division are appropriate,
we not only betray our calling but deny and wound the
heart of God. It is a matter of faithfulness for the church to
forgo the luxury of separate ways. A common path of unity
has been provided by God in Christ, who has made us one
so that the whole creation might be saved.

Epilogue

From Pittsburgh to Pittsburgh

Metaphorically, Pittsburgh will become the bookends for my active ministry as a United Methodist clergy. The General Conference held there in 1964 marked my initial entry in matters of the general church, as I stood with hundreds of others encircling the convention center in prayerful protest of the continuation of the Central Jurisdiction within our denominational structure. We were there to lobby for the elimination of this racist structure that belied our call to open the doors, spread the table, and end racial discrimination.

My memories of Pittsburgh 1964 are many, but one haunts me particularly. I left the picket line to find a bathroom inside the convention center. My age and arrogance destroyed the anonymity I sought. Delegates in the men's room knew what I represented and where I belonged, namely, outside. One said to me, "What are you doing here? Why don't you go back to where you came from and let us make the decisions we were elected to make?" My response was, "Yes, I know. You are here to oil the machinery, to keep it going as it is. Why don't you go back to your seat and do just that." Structurally, for four more hypocritical years, despite pious rhetoric to the contrary, we remained a segregated denomination in the name of timing, sensitivity, unity, and the coming merger with the Evangelical United Brethren Church.

As I begin to fold the umbrella of active ordained

ministry as the 2004 General Conference in Pittsburgh looms, I hear God in Christ asking me if I have been oiling the machinery of what exists while failing to employ a tough mind and tender heart, pastoral soul and a prophet's conscience for the kind of radical transformation that is conducive to the gospel and creates a Church that is a harbinger of God's kingdom/reign.

In response I affirm with humility and joy those occasions when I dared to follow the Risen Christ. But, shamefully and candidly, I confess and dissent from my own high blood pressure creeds that too often were followed by anemic deeds. I now realize how quickly time passes. Discipleship delayed is discipleship denied.

May Pittsburgh 2004 not be characterized by more oiling of the machinery of the status quo, but by the trust and obedience of hopeful and courageous progressive and neoliteralist United Methodists who, together with others, will dare to believe that this finite ecclesiastical system can still spread scriptural holiness across the land and around the globe. May we who will gather in Pittsburgh either enable it so to be, or at least to get out of the way so that God in Christ, working through others, will do just such a wondrous thing.

God can do this and more, so much more. Such are the affirmations of a dissenter.